AL CAPONE

AL CAPONE

A Biography

Luciano Iorizzo

GREENWOOD BIOGRAPHIES

GREENWOOD PRESS
WESTPORT, CONNECTICUT · LONDON

Library of Congress Cataloging-in-Publication Data

Iorizzo, Luciano J., 1930–
   Al Capone : a biography / Luciano Iorizzo.
       p. cm.—(Greenwood biographies, ISSN 1540–4900)
   Includes bibliographical references and index.
   ISBN 0–313–32317–8 (alk. paper)
       1. Capone, Al, 1899–1947. 2. Criminals—Illinois—Chicago—Biography. 3. Organized
   crime—Illinois—Chicago—History. I. Title. II. Series.
HV6248.C17I597   2003
364.1/092 B21   2003040824

British Library Cataloguing in Publication Data is available.

Library of Congress Catalog Card Number: 2003040824
ISBN: 0–313–32317–8
ISSN: 1540–4900

First published in 2003

Greenwood Press, 88 Post Road West, Westport, CT 06881
An imprint of Greenwood Publishing Group, Inc.
www.greenwood.com

Printed in the United States of America

The paper used in this book complies with the
Permanent Paper Standard issued by the National
Information Standards Organization (Z39.48–1984).

10   9   8   7   6   5   4   3

For Howard J. Williams, M.D.,
dedicated physician/surgeon, who knows how to treat skillfully
whole individuals and inspire them to get on with their lives.

CONTENTS

CONTENTS

Photo essay follows chapter 8

SERIES FOREWORD

In response to high school and public library needs, Greenwood developed this distinguished series of full-length biographies specifically for student use. Prepared by field experts and professionals, these engaging biographies are tailored for high school students who need challenging yet accessible biographies. Ideal for secondary school assignments, the length, format, and subject areas are designed to meet educators' requirements and students' interests.

Greenwood offers an extensive selection of biographies spanning all curriculum-related subject areas including social studies, the sciences, literature and the arts, history, and politics, as well as popular culture, covering public figures and famous personalities from all time periods and backgrounds, both historic and contemporary, who have made an impact on American and/or world culture. Greenwood biographies were chosen based on comprehensive feedback from librarians and educators. Consideration was given to both curriculum relevance and inherent interest. The result is an intriguing mix of the well known and the unexpected, the saints and sinners from long-ago history and contemporary pop culture. Readers will find a wide array of subject choices from fascinating crime figures like Al Capone to inspiring pioneers like Margaret Mead, from the greatest minds of our time like Stephen Hawking to the most amazing success stories of our day like J. K. Rowling.

While the emphasis is on fact, not glorification, the books are meant to be fun to read. Each volume provides in-depth information about the subject's life from birth through childhood, the teen years, and adulthood. A thorough account relates family background and education, traces personal and professional influences, and explores struggles, accomplishments, and contributions. A timeline highlights the most significant life events against a historical perspective. Suggestions for further reading give the biographies added reference value.

PREFACE

There has been much written about Al Capone. Indeed, one might wonder what could possibly be said about one of America's most identifiable criminals that has not already been documented. Most of the major writings have been done by journalists and others interested in crime. What seemed to be lacking was a perspective which included Italian American history and Organized Crime. This book seeks to remedy that situation.

Ethnicity, *diversity*, and *organized crime* are words bandied about freely in today's society. Minority groups are treated with a respect few thought possible or worth pursuing at the beginning of the twentieth century. The actions of minority groups, especially those from southern and eastern Europe, were prejudged to their detriment. This book gives the reader an opportunity to see Capone in a different light. It does not necessarily portray him in a better way, but certainly in a broader perspective. In an age which has come to view former radicals/criminals as benefactors for their group and society at large, readers can decide for themselves where Capone really fits in American society.

The author wishes to express his gratitude to many who helped make this book possible. Over the long haul, he has benefited from friends and colleagues too numerous to mention and from the many students who attended his courses in Immigration History and the History of Organized Crime. Their interest required this writer to stay current in his studies which often required fresh research. A number of individuals offered helpful advice on various themes in this book, read all or parts of the manuscript, and offered technical assistance in the use of the computer to get manuscripts ready for publication. Among them are Dr. Joel Swerdlow, a

xii PREFACE

former student and presently a Washington, D.C. based author and professor; Bruce Frassinelli, retired publisher of the *Oswego Palladium-Times*; Dr. Judith Gusweiler, psychologist; and James Patridge, a school counselor skilled in computer expertise. Special thanks to Impressions Book and Journal Services for getting the book to market in a timely fashion. I am most indebted to Kevin Ohe, sponsoring editor of this book. He has shepherded me from day one. He helped to keep me focused on the readership, provided invaluable suggestions to improve the overall thrust of the book, and never failed to make better, when needed, the turn of a phrase. As always, my wife, Martha Marilee, was there for me. A lifelong inspiration, she encouraged me, read the manuscript, and offered helpful criticism. For any errors in fact or judgment, I, alone, am responsible.

Luciano J. Iorizzo

INTRODUCTION

Al Capone! He has been dead for more than 50 years, yet he continues to draw the attention of people worldwide, more so perhaps than any other Italian American and most Americans. What makes him one of America's most enduring and infamous characters is open to debate. His rap sheet was not unlike that of many common criminals. It included arrests for traffic violations (dismissed), disorderly conduct (dismissed), and operating a house of prostitution. He was charged with gambling (fined $150), carrying a concealed weapon (discharged), and violation of prohibition (twice, dismissed). He was booked for voting fraud (dismissed) and suspicion of murder (twice, dismissed). He was fined for carrying a concealed weapon in Joliet, Illinois, and, on another occasion, he served time in Pennsylvania on a similar offense. Miami police took him in on various vagrancy, suspicion, and perjury charges, which did not hold up in court. The entry on income tax evasion, of course, listed his conviction, for which he received an eleven-year sentence. This record hardly warrants his being counted among the world's most ruthless killers, an animal feared by his cohorts and ordinary citizens, a gang leader held responsible for corrupting the processes of law enforcement, legislative bodies, and the judicial system. In fact, the deed that brought him the longest prison term was actually a white collar crime, a crime that seldom leads to incarceration. But the media paid little mind to legal niceties in the 1920s. Starting then and continuing thereafter, reporters, radio commentators, and filmmakers both demonized and glamorized Al Capone. There was little that went wrong in Chicago in his heyday for which he was not blamed. The media made him out to be a "superstar" of the underworld.[1]

Capone became larger than life and loved every minute of it. The U.S. government, whose quixotic Prohibition policy gave rise to bootlegging gangs throughout the land, helped create Al Capone, Public Enemy Number One.[2] But Capone himself must take most of the responsibility. He played his role to the hilt. Taking advantage of every opportunity to publicize himself, he willingly talked with reporters. Never admitting to murder or running brothels, he offered himself as a businessman supplying a product eagerly sought by consumers. The fact that the product was illegal alcohol made no difference to him. He rationalized that so many good citizens ignored the Volstead Act, which made it illegal to manufacture, sell, transport, import, and export intoxicating beverages, that he should not be singled out for giving the populace what it craved. After all, he argued, many policemen, judges, and legislators drank. Technically, it wasn't illegal to do so.[3] His argument was self-serving, but not without some merit. It has gained more credibility as the years have passed.

The erroneous notion, held by many people, that links Capone with the Mafia should not be overlooked. Since the late nineteenth century Americans have had a fascination with the Mafia, with which they have equated Italian American criminals.[4] This helped to make Capone an even more irresistible attraction. People have never tired of reading books, watching movies, viewing videos, and tuning into television shows that deal with Al Capone, directly or indirectly, in which fictionalized mobsters were thinly disguised portrayals of Scarface Al.[5] This attention has exaggerated his role in organized crime. Being of Neapolitan extraction, he was not eligible for Mafia membership (if indeed, that Western Sicilian organization existed in the United States). Still, one can hardly describe Capone as simply involved in what is termed today *victimless crime*. He fits somewhere between what the public has been led to believe all these years, what the record shows, and how he fashioned himself.

Capone remains one of the most interesting criminals in history whose story continues to fascinate people from all walks of life. Like Tony Soprano today of HBO's *The Sopranos*, a fictional gang leader and killer, who has gained and kept the attention of millions of television viewers, Capone continues to capture the imagination of millions of Americans through books, magazine articles, television, and the movies. He turns up in the most unlikely places. In 1997, a book on Italian humor, which featured such classic authors as Giovanni Boccaccio, Dante, Alessandro Manzoni, Cesare Beccaria, and a host of others, included five humorous sayings from Al Capone.[6] After the tragedy of the bombing of the World Trade Center in 2001, Capone was mentioned in various news broadcasts. In one, an American commentator referred to him to demonstrate the inhumanity of the attack. In another, a Taliban spokesman used him to show that the terrorists' actions weren't so horrible when put into a Caponian context.

It is no easy chore, though it is extremely intriguing, to separate the fantasy from the reality in the life of Al Capone. Many authors, struck by the frightening violence of the 1920s, portray Capone as the prime villain, the most violent, insensitive, wanton killer of his time. Despite the lack of courtroom proof, there seems to be little disagreement that Capone was a murderer, brothel-keeper, bootlegger, gambler, and gang leader. Viewing that period from a distance, some writers today are apt to be somewhat sympathetic. While not apologists for Capone, these authors see him as a product of his times, as much responding to violence and corruption as initiating it. They recognize that he helped the needy. They view him as a family man who believed in old-fashioned values. They remark on his devotion to his mother, brothers, sister, son, and extended family. And difficult as it is to fathom, though he pimped and chased women, they cite the mutual devotion that he and his wife, Mae, shared.[7]

It is what is not in the official record that gives Capone his historic authenticity. His conviction record to the contrary, the media portrayed Capone as a brutal, beastly murderer who ruthlessly eliminated his competition. Sometimes he was given credit for pulling the trigger himself or battering his opponents to death. Other times, as in the St. Valentine's Day slaughter, he was identified as the one ordering his henchmen to do the dastardly deed while he basked in the sun in Florida. The newspapers also marked him as a pimp, running a number of brothels in Cook County. For Capone's part, he never knew what all the fuss was about. He owned up to gambling and supplying Chicagoans with alcohol, activities that an overwhelming number of its citizens either approved of or craved. He could see nothing wrong with that. But, claiming a deep devotion to family values, he denied participating in activities involving murder and prostitution.

Al Capone, also known as Scarface, the Big Fellow, Al Brown, and assorted other names, didn't understand that outside the big cities was a different world, an Anglo-Saxon Protestant one where many people viewed drinking and card-playing (to say nothing of gambling) as sinful. He did not realize that there were relatively few Catholics in the United States beyond the Irish, who were essentially urbanites. Nor could he know that the Catholic Church still considered most of the United States missionary territory. Perhaps it is that naïveté, that disarming charm, maybe a feigned innocence, that drew people to him; or his generosity, his concern for the downtrodden, his gregariousness. Maybe it was his opulent lifestyle: the custom-made automobiles with bulletproof glass and armor-plated steel, or parading around town with flashy women at his side under the protection of bodyguards, or the tailored suits in colors associated with pimps on Times Square and the pearl-colored fedoras. Perhaps Capone was the symbol of hope for the downtrodden in the Depression. While Americans early on felt the sting of a worldwide economic slide, Capone reveled in his glory, feeding the poor in soup kitchens and being living proof for those who hoped that prosperity was just around the corner. Some likened him to Jesse James, a murderer and thief, who came to be a hero in nineteenth-century rural America. As America developed in the twentieth century, Al Capone became James's counterpart in urban America. People still disagree on James. Some see him as a villain. Others claim him as an authentic American Robin Hood. History can at times whitewash the evil deeds of the past. Putting things in perspective has a way of doing that. Was Capone the innocent he claimed to be? Was he the epitome of evil, as his detractors claim? Was he the greatest gangster the world has ever known, as some have claimed? Was he the de facto ruler of Chicago? Or has his influence and role in that city been exaggerated? Moreover, what has been his status in organized crime? Has history been accurate on Capone? We shall see.

NOTES

1. Capone's offenses are readily available in a number of books, but see Laurence Bergreen, *Capone: The Man and The Era* (New York, 1994), pp. 661–62.

2. Frank J. Loesch, head of the Chicago Crime Commission, originated a list of public enemies in Chicago in 1930 and defined Al Capone as Public Enemy Number One. See Bergreen, *Capone: The Man*, pp. 366–67. H.L. Mencken, *The American Language*, Supplement II (New York, 1962), p. 672 states that Homer S. Cummings, Attorney General of the United States from 1933–39, coined the phrase, which was used to classify national criminals. On that level, John Dillinger was the original Public Enemy Number One.

3. Fred D. Pasley, *Al Capone: The Biography of a Self-Made Man* (1930; reprint, Freeport, N.Y., 1971), pp. 349–55.

4. See, for example, Luciano J. Iorizzo and Salvatore Mondello, *The Italian Americans*, rev. ed. (Boston, 1980), pp. 184–215; and Luciano J. Iorizzo, "Crime and Organized Crime," in *The Italian American Experience: An Encyclopedia*, ed. Salvatore J. LaGumina, et al. (New York, 2000), pp. 151–59.

5. Iorizzo and Mondello, *Italian Americans*, rev. ed., pp. 269 ff. See also the list of movies and videos in the bibliography at the end of this book.

6. Henry D. Spalding, *Joys of Italian Humor* (New York, 1997).

7. See, for example, Martin Short, *Crime Inc.: The Story of Organized Crime* (London, 1984), pp. 84–87.

TIMELINE

1894 Gabriele and Teresa Capone immigrate to the United States with sons Vincenzo (Richard James "Two Gun" Hart) and Raffaele James (Ralph "Bottles").

1895 Salvatore F. (Frank) Capone born in January.

1899 Alphonse (Al) Capone born in Brooklyn.

1901 Erminio (John, Mimi) Capone born.

1906 Umberto (Albert) Capone born.

1908 Amedio (Matthew N.) Capone born.

1909 Johnny Torrio goes to Chicago.

1910 Rose Capone born and dies.

1912 Mafalda Capone born.

1917 Capone hired as bouncer in the Harvard Inn, Coney Island, and gets three scars on his face.

1918 Capone's son, Albert Francis (Sonny) born on December 4. Sometime prior to Sonny's birth, Capone probably contracted syphilis. On December 30, Capone marries Mary Josephine (Mae) Coughlin, mother of Sonny.

1919 Capone quits working for Yale and becomes a legitimate bookkeeper for Aiello Construction in Baltimore. Torrio opens the Four Deuces. The Prohibition Amendment (18th) passed into law on October 28.

1920 Volstead Act takes effect on January 19. Big Jim Colosimo killed in Chicago on May 11. Gabriele Capone, Al's father, dies on November 14.

1921 Capone arrives in Chicago and works for Johnny Torrio.

1922   Ralph Capone arrives in Chicago and works vice for Johnny Torrio. Capone arrested in August for DWI, carrying a concealed weapon, and assault with an automobile; the charges are dropped.

1922–1923   Capone promoted to manager of the Four Deuces.

1923   William Dever becomes mayor of Chicago in April. Capone taken in as a partner by Johnny Torrio and seeks to distance himself from prostitution. Capone's wife, son, mother, other brothers, and sister join him in Chicago; all except Ralph live in his house at 7244 Prairie Avenue. Torrio moves operations to Cicero in October. In the fall, Torrio convinces other gangsters to cooperate peacefully in dividing up the rackets in Cicero, then takes his mother to Italy and resettles her there. Capone takes over in Cicero while Torrio is away.

1924   Torrio returns in the spring. Frank Capone killed during Cicero's elections in April. Joe Howard killed (presumably by Capone) on May 8. Torrio arrested on May 19 on Prohibition charge at the Sieben Brewery double-cross by Dion O'Banion. Eddie Tancl killed in November. Dion O'Banion killed (presumably on orders of Torrio, Capone, and/or the Genna Brothers) on November 10.

1925   Failed attempt on Capone's life on January 12, and Torrio seriously wounded and hospitalized on January 24, in retaliation for the O'Banion murder. Torrio fined and sentenced to nine months in jail on February 9 for Sieben Prohibition offense; Capone is left in charge while Torrio is in jail. When Torrio is released, he turns leadership over to Capone and leaves Chicago. Angelo Genna killed on May 26. Michael Genna killed on June 13. Anthony Genna killed on July 8. Samuzzo "Samoots" Amatuna killed on November 13.

1926   William McSwiggin, assistant state's attorney, killed on April 27. Weiss and company rake Hawthorne Hotel in Cicero with 5,000 rounds of ammo on September 20. Weiss killed on October 11. Truce declared in meeting at Morrison Hotel on November 21.

1927   Frank "Lefty" Koncil killed on March 11. Failed attempt on Capone's life at Hot Springs, Arkansas, on March 14, probably by Vincent "The Schemer" Drucci in reprisal for the Weiss slaying. Drucci killed by police on April 4. Capone visits Los Angeles and is run out of town around December 6. Capone arrested and fined $2,600 for a concealed weapon charge in Joliet, Ill., on December 22.

1928   Capone goes to Miami, then Miami Beach, on January 4, where he takes a hotel room and leases a house for his wife and family. Capone buys Palm Isle house on Biscayne Bay on March 27. Frankie Yale killed on July 8. Jack Zuta killed on August 1. Arnold Rothstein killed on December 4. All Sicilian criminals' conference held in Cleveland on December 5.

1929   St. Valentine's Day massacre on February 14 while Capone is in Florida. Murder of Anselmi, Scalise, and Guinta on May 7. Atlantic City Gangland Conference held from May 13 to 16. Capone arrested in Philadelphia on May 17 for a concealed weapon and on May 18 was given one year in prison at Eastern State Penitentiary, his first jail sentence.

1930   Capone released on March 17 after serving his sentence. Capone arrested in Miami several times in May for suspicion, vagrancy, and perjury, all dismissed. Capone feeds indigents in his Chicago soup kitchens in December.

1931   Joe "The Boss" Masseria killed on April 15. Capone indicted on June 5 on 22 counts of income tax evasion; later, on June 12, he is indicted on Prohibition violations as well. Meeting in Cleveland, possibly in July, to eliminate Maranzano, reorganize gangs to cooperate, and Americanize without any "boss of bosses." Salvatore Maranzano killed on September 10. Capone's income tax trial begins on October 6; he is found guilty on five counts of tax evasion on October 17 and, on October 24, sentenced to 11 years in prison and fined $50,000 and court costs of $30,000. The indictment for violation of Prohibition is dropped.

1932   Appeals denied on May 3; Capone begins sentence in Atlanta Penitentiary.

1933   Prohibition Amendment repealed.

1934   Capone transferred to Alcatraz on August 19.

1939   Capone transferred to Terminal Island, south of Los Angeles, on January 6. Informant Ed O'Hare killed on November 8. Capone transferred to Lewisburg Penitentiary, Pa., on November 13 for release. Capone paroled on November 16.

1939   Dr. Moore begins treatments for Capone's syphilis at Union Hospital, Baltimore, on November 17.

Chapter 1

MAFIA, BLACK HAND, AND ORGANIZED CRIME: THE BEGINNINGS OF A NATIONAL SYNDICATE

Many Americans too often lump together the terms *Mafia*, *Black Hand*, and *organized crime* as if they were synonymous. In the confusion, they often erroneously associate Al Capone with the Mafia. This is due to the fact that in the effort to simplify, many sources deal inadequately with the subject. The media, through the press, pulp fiction, movies, videos, and so-called documentaries, are especially guilty of taking an uncritical approach in favor of a popular one. So the misconceptions live. A brief objective look at these organizations can shed some light on their nature and on Capone's role in them.

First, one must deal with the duality of the Mafia. The Mafia had its origins in western Sicily, where landowners recruited "troops" to protect themselves, their homes, and their families from marauding bands and the extortionate foreigners who had invaded their country and ruled over them. They collected "taxes" from those who wanted protection from the foreign rulers. Thus, young women who were attacked, the weak who were trammeled, the men of respect who were mistreated came to find a swifter and more equitable form of justice in the local Mafia society than what the so-called legitimate governments offered. This system evolved into an association of small, loosely organized criminal bands (*cosche*) that specialized in cattle rustling, extortion, and kidnapping. Members of the group took the oath of *omertà*, which bound them never to apply for justice to legally constituted bodies or to assist in the detection of crime. Each band took its members from its home town. Outsiders, even Sicilians from another community, were not trusted. If the *cosche* were ever betrayed, it had to be by one of their own members. This was highly unlikely. Thus, a movement, not criminal at its inception, contained the seeds wherefrom clandestine associations could and did emerge. What made the Mafia work in Sicily was its complete immersion in the native society. Anyone from any walk of life might be involved in it for themselves or for the good of the oppressed.

When Italians refer to the Mafia in Sicily, the vast majority of them do not take offense. They understand that the Mafia is a sub-group, just as Americans would not feel personally maligned if one were to write about criminals in America. In contrast, when one writes of the Mafia in America, one refers to more than a criminal class. One describes alleged alien conspirators who have for decades been so liberally identified that few Italian Americans can escape the stigma completely. As early as 1888, the *Chicago Tribune* argued somewhat startlingly that Chicago must have a Mafia because where there are Sicilians there is also a Mafia. Since many Italians in Chicago were Sicilians, Chicago had a Mafia. Two years later, Chief of Police David C. Hennessy of New Orleans was murdered. Italians were blamed. Americans were told of an alleged conspiracy to assassinate public officials who would not do the bidding of the Mafia. The implication was clear that politicians and government officials were controlled by criminals, not vice-versa. America's sovereignty was being threatened. This was a heavy burden to which citizens throughout the nation were exposed. They were frightened and made sensitive to the potential for destruction that the alleged Mafia posed. The stereotype was reinforced in the early twentieth century by a congressional report in general and E.A. Ross in particular. Ross was one of America's preeminent sociologists. He charged that Sicilians were primitive and ferocious people.[1] Other writers concluded that Southern Italians were criminally inclined, "dishonest, hot-blooded, ignorant and dirty."[2] Though these misconceptions were eventually abandoned by most scholars and thinking people, the damage had been done. The criminal stigma stuck. Burned into the minds of most Americans, the criminal label remains in the twenty-first century, though weakened. Moreover, little thought was ever given to how a criminal group, if indeed it wanted to transplant itself, could immerse itself and survive in a society that had a different language, set of customs, and religion. Could what took centuries to develop in Sicily work in America overnight? Undoubtedly, Italian criminals came to America. Even mafiosi did. But eventually they became Americanized, and that included their criminal ways. Johnny Torrio, Al Capone, Lucky Luciano, and others would move Italians into the system of organized crime they found in America. They would help refine it, improve on it, expand its scope nationwide.

Exacerbating the problem for these immigrants was the fact that they were viewed by Americans as Italians, a monolithic group. In reality, Italy had only recently become a modern nation. Its people were proud of their regional ancestry. They viewed themselves as Sicilians, Neapolitans, Romans, and so on. But they were part of a class system, economically rooted, in which northerners took preeminence over southerners and relegated Sicilians to the lowest ranks. Neapolitans who scorned the condescending attitudes and actions directed against them by their northern brethren were just as quick in denigrating their countrymen farther south. Even in America, the Sicilians were ostracized by other Italians, who believed them to be of non-Italian and even savage origins. The important point for understanding the Mafia is that Americans believed the immigrants from Italy were a cohesive Italian group. Americans failed to understand the distinctions between Sicilians, Neapolitans, Romans, and so on. *Mafia* was applied indiscriminately and erroneously to all Italians regardless of their origins. Such a notion made critical examination of the Mafia all but impossible.

Shortly after the Mafia was making headlines in America, the Black Hand hysteria hit the nation. It hit in the late 1800s, when the masses from southern Italy began seeking economic betterment in America. Virtually none of them could speak English. They were conspicuous. They had few connections to American institutions. Indeed, they found it hard to join any group on an equal-member basis. Under these conditions, the few that were criminally inclined were best suited to, if not limited to, taking advantage of their own kind. Black Hand extortionists were an example of this sort of criminal activity. They terrorized their fellow immigrants. The masses suffered these indignities until they learned that local police and federal forces could protect them against criminal intimidation. Soon, many respectable Italians cooperated with law enforcement. Before Prohibition came about in 1920, the Black Hand had been eliminated. By then, talk of the Mafia had also died out. In fact, the word *Mafia* virtually disappeared from the lexicon throughout the entire Prohibition period. It was not until after World War II that it burst on the scene, despite the rise in the 1920s of the one man most connected to Italian American crime, Al Capone. But he was no mafioso. Later and erroneously, Americans caught up in Mafia hysteria associated him with the Mafia. By then, the fact that it was possible to have Italian Americans involved in organized crime without a Mafia was never considered.

In sum, Black Hand crimes were a form of extortion characterized by using the anonymous threatening letter. Potential victims were told to pay or die. Bombings of businesses often followed those slow to pay. For more than 15 years, Italian criminals and members of other national groups using the same modus operandi terrified those who had money. When Italians had confidence that the local police were not in league with the extortionists, they cooperated and helped bring the Black Handers to justice. But in the end it was the federal government that eliminated such crimes by prosecuting those using the mail for their nefarious practices.

As organized crime began to develop in the early twentieth century, it depended on an intricate interrelationship between many elements in a society that kept the likes of newcomer Italians in a low place in the total structure. Syndicates, or organized crime sectors, were organized like political machines, and in some cases were indistinguishable from political organizations. It was not unusual for syndicate members to hold office in a party structure or even be elected to a local or state governmental position. Italians were seldom able to be in a position to run for public office. Having newly come to America, they, including the criminal element among them, were on the outside looking in. What they saw often were immigrants who preceded them by a generation or two moving into the system. The Irish fit in best, but Germans and Jews were also noticeably present. Prohibition gave the Italians their big opportunity. Al Capone was there in the beginning. He had a chance to become a major player as an independent and a national syndicate boss. He was to succeed as the former but not the latter.

Mafia, Black Hand, and *organized crime* are clearly three distinct concepts. Making them synonymous makes it difficult to understand the role of people like Al Capone and organized crime in America. The case of Jim Colosimo is instructive. He was a wealthy criminal with plenty of political support who was a prime target of Black Hand extortionists. If organized crime was the monolithic creation people have made it out to be, Colosimo would have been free of such threats. But such was not the case. Italian criminals were prime targets for extortionists because they had money. The fact that Black Handers threatened gang leaders indicates that the extortionists did not consider them to be powerful enough to worry about. Possibly they didn't understand with whom they were dealing. Whatever the case, the machinations of the Black Handers are ample testimony to the lack of solidarity between them and the so-called Mafia.

Though successful in pimping and gambling, Colosimo owed his position to politicians. Like all successful criminals, he was their lackey, not their boss. Torrio and Capone, for all their power, were no different. They existed by the approval of the politicians and governmental officials. And so it is with all organized crime figures. They are taken down when their reach exceeds what is allowed them. As we shall see, both constituted authority and organized crime leaders concluded, at about the same time, that Al Capone had gone too far.

Though the term *Black Hand* has passed from common usage, *Mafia* and *organized crime* remain. Because Italian Americans had been tainted with the label of criminality, they became synonymous with *Mafia*, which, in turn, became one and the same with organized crime. Given that, many people concluded that Italians equaled organized crime and organized crime equaled Italians. Even the U.S. government came to take the official position that organized crime and the Mafia—that is, the Italian American criminal—were one and the same. Despite the government's retreat from that position, many people still hold to it. The fact that it was possible to have Italian Americans involved in organized crime without a Mafia has seldom been considered. Nor can many people envision organized crime existing without Italian Americans despite the considerable evidence that shows multi-ethnic involvement in it. Though primarily a major independent, Capone had some involvement with organized crime, and his outfit's personnel were decidedly well diversified.

Organized crime is based on satisfying consumer needs. It rests on centuries of interactions between people who would circumvent the law to satisfy their desires. Unlike the criminal who forces victims to give in to his or her demands, organized crime figures usually find willing participants eager to avail themselves of the illegal services. This system developed from the colonists' wishes to justify actions against what they considered an irrelevant or oppressive rule from a distant mother country. In time, American society allowed for a dual existence, one that legislated ideal social and moral values, and another that permitted, unofficially, deviation from the codes.

Trying to bring an ideal society into existence through laws presented enormous problems for officials. Inasmuch as it was nearly impossible to have the real world coincide with the ideal one, officials had to decide which laws to take seriously and which ones to overlook but occasionally enforce for appearances' sake. What came about was a mechanism to control but not eliminate the illicit activities. In the nineteenth century, activities kept under check by the law were gambling, prostitution, and bootleg liquor. Yet early on, politicians and police were the first large-scale criminal entrepreneurs, owning and operating gambling halls and brothels that were often combined under one roof. Having control over the police, politicians were the senior partners in such ventures. Later, they began "licensing" their illegal operations to gang leaders. By the 1890s, Americans had a hard time distinguishing between politicians and criminals, between lawmen and thugs. It was into this society that the masses of Italian immigrants came. A ready-made criminal world awaited any of them who were so inclined. Still, Americans continued to blame the immigrants for crime. Colonists who settled in early America blamed those who came after them for outbreaks of crime. In the nineteenth century, Americans believed first the Irish to be the main source of criminality, then the Germans, the Jews, and the Italians, along with African Americans. It was an easy way of avoiding responsibility for a system they established that encouraged law-breaking. The roots of organized crime, which ran deep in American soil, were ignored. It was better to blame the immigrants for carrying this "plague" to America.[3]

NOTES

1. Cited in Luciano J. Iorizzo and Salvatore Mondello, *The Italian Americans*, rev. ed. (Boston, 1980), p. 189.

2. Ibid.

3. See ibid., pp. 184–215; Luciano J. Iorizzo, "Crime and Organized Crime," in *The Italian American Experience: An Encyclopedia*, ed. Salvatore J. LaGumina, et al. (New York, 2000), pp. 151–59.

Chapter 2

URBAN CESSPOOLS: GANGS AND POLITICIANS

The United States in the 1890s was midway in a transition period going from an agricultural nation to a modern industrial society. As Americans left farms for the cities, many citizens lamented that fact. Though they did not become overwhelmingly hostile to urban values, they reflected the Jeffersonian notion that cities were moral cesspools and farms were the strongholds of virtue. Moreover, the closing of the frontier, celebrated by Frederick Jackson Turner in 1893, made Americans wonder if Thomas Jefferson had been right in warning about the materialism, commercialism, corruption, and evil influences of European cities taking root in America.[1]

Jefferson was in the vanguard of those who ascribed America's shortcomings to the foreigners. America did become materialistic, commercial, and industrial, and it had its fair share of evil. But it would be hard to lay these developments at the foot of European immigrants. In the criminal milieu, which is the major concern of this book, American culture has been reluctant to own up to its own role. Al Capone was not an Italian. He was American born. He was raised in a country that had a duality of life. There was a set of laws that showed its citizens to be virtuous and morally upright. America was mostly Protestant. People were proud of that, proud to stand for hard work and clean living. Its laws were testimony to that. Gambling was illegal. Prostitution was not allowed. Drugs—opium, for example—were seen as an anomaly practiced by Chinese immigrants and eventually outlawed. Consumption of alcoholic beverages was proscribed in many communities before national prohibition. On the surface, America provided an ideal environment where one could raise a family free from the enervating vices that have plagued mankind from time immemorial. Beneath the surface, things were not so simple. Some of the legislators who passed the laws, and the executives and police charged with enforcing them, were the very same people who violated the legislation and benefited handsomely from doing so. Many of the judges were just as guilty as the politicians.

The American people were at the heart of the problem. Enough of them wanted their pleasures. They wanted to drink, gamble, and carouse. This created a dilemma for society. Many of the public officials involved in legislation and enforcement either saw nothing wrong with so-called victimless crimes or saw the futility of trying to enforce such laws in a society that demanded such services. Furthermore, if they persisted in bringing victimless crime's lawbreakers to justice, they ran the risk of being turned out at the next election. In retaliation, the voters would elect officials more sympathetic to their lifestyles. Each community had to handle its own problems. The opportunity for enrichment was enormous. The community could benefit from payments given to it for allowing and controlling an illegal activity for the public good. But public officials could take many actions to enrich themselves. They could own and operate these illicit businesses outright. They could simply have gangsters front for them. And, as the years went on, more and more of the elected and appointed public servants preferred to receive payoffs from gangsters who owned and operated the gambling joints and brothels. In New Orleans, politicians opted for establishing a red-light district to control prostitution. The income from such an arrangement went to charitable causes, not into the pockets of any individuals. The system worked well until the Secretary of the Navy closed the brothels during World War I as a way to protect servicemen from venereal disease, which threatened the military to a large extent. The route taken in New Orleans example was the exception to the rule. It was mostly venal public officials who tackled the problem with their own welfare in mind. They enriched themselves as up-front operators or "silent partners." They lived in an age when public servants were expected to take advantage of their chances when they came along. Clearly, this was the case in most communities throughout the nation, especially in New York and Chicago.[2]

At the time Capone was growing up in Brooklyn, New York City was caught up in one of its worst police corruption sagas ever. It could hardly have been unexpected. Since the 1820s, New York City had been developing a municipal system based on corruption. Aided by thugs who formed various gangs, party leaders fought for control. Neighborhood hoodlums stuffed ballot boxes; voted repeatedly, even using names of deceased people; and discouraged suspected opposition voters from entering the polling booths. Winning elections meant controlling the police force, which sometimes would be completely replaced if a rival party took over. It also gave the victors control over vice operations, mainly prostitution and gambling, which supplied a good deal of the campaign funds and money to supplement the salaries of public officials. Oftentimes, before a brothel or gambling establishment was allowed to open, a substantial sum would be required up front. Thereafter, the public officials, police included, had a share of the illegal business and/or took either a set amount or a percentage of the profits in payoffs. From time to time, when public pressure demanded, raids would be staged to give the impression of alert and effective policing. Inasmuch as a great number of New Yorkers availed themselves of illegal services, reform movements, if successful, were generally short-lived. In essence, graft and corruption became a way of life. Boss William Tweed's ring is the most noted example of municipal mismanagement. But it is the varied career of John Morrissey that is more relevant to our story.

The Morrissey family, including John and his seven sisters, left Ireland and hoped to improve the family fortunes in Canada in 1834. Becoming destitute there, they moved to Troy, New York, after three months. His father found enough work to keep the family going. Young John Morrissey got a job as a bartender when he was still a teenager. A self-taught street fighter who loved to challenge anyone when he drank too much, he was very much at home with his clientele consisting of gamblers, thieves, and assorted riffraff. By age 18 he had already established a reputation as a local gang leader and been indicted numerous times for burglary, assault with intent to kill, and assault and battery. When the Gold Rush took place in California, he made his way west, hoping to box his way to riches in that rough-and-tumble country if panning for gold did not succeed. Neither activity worked out. His love for fighting moved him to turn professional and settle in New York City, where the big money action was. His strength, determination, and driving desire served him well. He beat Yankee Sullivan to lay claim to the heavyweight title in 1853. It was a grueling 37-round match, which netted him $2,000. In 1858, challenged by John C. Heenan, Morrissey took only 11 rounds to retain his title. He earned $2,500 for his efforts and decided to retire as world champion and devote his talents to business and politics. In between the championship bouts, one of Morrissey's opponents was murdered. Morrissey was arrested on suspicion of murder, but eventually released.

Aware of Morrissey's criminal background, Captain Isaiah Rynders, a rising Tammany leader of dubious background, saw the potential value of the former prize-fighter. He did not disappoint Tammany. Using his muscle and ability to organize repeaters at the polls for Boss Tweed, he gained a reputation par excellence that the media and the opposition spread widely. In appreciation, Rynders and Boss Tweed gave Morrissey the political protection he needed to carve out a remarkable career for himself.

By the Civil War, Morrissey had become the city's premier gambler. But he wanted more than that. His ambition drove him to expand his gambling operations to Saratoga Springs in 1861, where he eventually opened a casino that catered to the blue bloods of America's political, military, and industrial elite. Though he was clearly known as a gambler and deeply involved in voting irregularities, he won a seat in the House of Representatives from the Fifth New York District. He served two terms in Washington, which allowed him to expand his gambling activities where he had a share in a casino-type establishment in the nation's capital. In 1875 and again in 1877, Morrissey won election to New York's State Senate. The following year, while in office, his life was cut short by pneumonia.

When he died, he owned significant shares in the racetrack and its buildings at Saratoga, a major gambling casino there, as well as many parcels of real estate scattered around the city. State senators acted as pallbearers. He was mourned by many who looked behind his gruff exterior to his kindheartedness and loyalty to friends who came from all walks of life, blue bloods like Commodore Vanderbilt and commoners alike. Upwards of 15,000 people braved the rain to join the funeral cortege to the cemetery. Though he reportedly made and lost fortunes on Wall Street, his estate was valued between $40,000 and $250,000.[3]

Morrissey was, among other things, a businessman, gambler, and politician. His story is just one of many that illuminate the interrelationships between gamblers, thugs, police, politicians, and the leaders of the industrial-business complex who sought ways to circumvent the restrictive legislation that hampered those looking for good times. It also makes it easier to understand how the tragic tale of police lieutenant Charles Becker could ever come to pass.

With a loan of $1,500 from Lieutenant Becker, Herman Rosenthal opened a gambling house in midtown Manhattan. The conditions stipulated that Rosenthal take in as a partner Becker's surrogate, one Jack Rose. Becker's cut would be 25 percent of the profits. Such propositions were extremely profitable for the police lieutenant who, at one time, had deposited close to $60,000 in his savings account when his salary was less than $2,000 a year. Getting greedy, Becker sought to up his take from Rosenthal, who balked. Subsequently, the heat was put on gambling in the city, and Becker asked Rosenthal to make a raid, which was a normal action by the police to mask their involvement with gambling and vice operations. Rosenthal refused and went public with what he felt was police extortion. In retaliation, Becker hired four assassins to kill Rosenthal. A jury found Becker and the four killers guilty. The state electrocuted all of them at Sing Sing prison.[4]

In the 1840s, Chicago was a frontier town. Gambling was illegal, yet the authorities encouraged it. Professional gamblers, with the help of saloon keepers and hack drivers (precursors to cab drivers), made gaming available to all. Private clubs catered to the respectable and wealthy. The police, who owed their jobs to whomever was in office, came under the control of political parties, whichever one happened to be in power at the time. For the next 100 years and more, law enforcement was hampered by political control. If a public official had a piece of the action, the police were powerless to interfere. In time, the police themselves would share in the payoffs. This was the way it was across America's cities.[5] But Chicago was to become synonymous with police corruption. In essence, Chicago became a wide-open city early on. The voters willingly elected mayoral candidates who openly espoused accommodation with the underworld. More than a few reform mayors, honest men, had relatively little success in changing permanently the face of the city. If they were too successful, the electorate voted them out at the next election.

It was Michael Cassius McDonald who championed the concept of a wide-open Chicago and set the foundations for what we call organized crime today. Able to unify the Irish during the Civil War, he rose from street hustler to gambler to political boss, creating Chicago's first effective political machine. Gambling profits enabled him to finance the careers of many politicians, and his gambling house became the headquarters for top city officials. He was instrumental in forming a bookmaking syndicate, which operated at racetracks in Illinois and Indiana. His alliances with politicians provided a model for gamblers throughout the nation to carry on their illegal business with official approval. Ever mindful of upward social mobility and the drive for respectability, he purchased the *Chicago Globe* and became treasurer of the Elevated Railroad Company. McDonald, in short, became a power in Chicago, strong enough to get mayors elected. And if some gamblers or pimps were slow to get behind his man, he saw to it that the police closed their businesses.

McDonald's success attracted competition. But what did him in were marriage difficulties. His first wife deserted him. His second wife shocked him by allegedly shooting to death a young man with whom she was having an affair. McDonald had a nervous breakdown and eventually died on August 9, 1907. Though his role in corrupting life in Chicago was recognized, the press admitted that newcomers were drawn to the city because it was wide open. The atmosphere McDonald created was instrumental in providing the spark that helped the city attract new citizens and develop it into a growing, thriving metropolis, crooked deals and all. Given this background, is it any wonder that others, years later, would view Capone as a positive force in Chicago, or that Capone himself would say seriously, "I'm just a businessman who supplies people with what they want to buy, in the good old American way"?[6]

Beyond that, it was McDonald's contribution to the development of criminal associations that stands out. McDonald provided a working model whereby gamblers and assorted felons could practice their trades in some organized manner with a minimum of violence. Early on he demonstrated the benefits of organizing criminal activities. Those who came after him were not blind to the model he left them or to the business opportunities he opened for them. A prime example is that of the career of Big Jim Colosimo.

Colosimo was a Calabrian immigrant who came to Chicago via a railroad section gang.[7] This was a common way that Italian immigrants, aided by padrone agents working hand in hand with the railroads, gained the mobility to travel the nation and settle wherever they desired. The railroads played a key role in helping immigrants form distribution patterns in America. They employed Italian padrone agents to locate immigrants in Italy and escort them to seaports on the East Coast of the United States, usually New York City. There many immigrants joined railroad gangs and worked their way across the country under the tutelage of the padrones.[8] Like so many travelers who came to Chicago, Colosimo saw the opportunities it presented and settled there. He started out as a street-sweeper, organized his fellow Italians into a political bloc in the First Ward, and caught the attention of Aldermen John "Bathhouse" Coughlin and Michael "Hinky Dink" Kenna, who made Colosimo a precinct captain for the Democrats. Coughlin and Kenna were colorful political bosses of the First Ward who controlled prostitution and other criminal activity there. Their trademark was a bawdy, dissolute, orgiastic annual ball which drew overflow crowds of those who felt compelled to purchase tickets lest their brothels and gambling establishments would feel the powerful arm of the law controlled by the two "Lords of the Levee," as they became known. Wearing masks to conceal their identities, many respectable people participated in these raucous fund-raisers. The event had a revival in 1973, and the *New York Times* reported on October 16, 1973, that a highlight of the ball was the performance of the Al Capone Memorial Jazz Band, fitting in that Capone was a jazz enthusiast and supporter while in Chicago.

Colosimo quickly sensed that the balance of power in city government was held by the underworld. He became the first Italian to head a criminal association, or syndicate, as many in the illegal business of vice, gambling, and peddling illicit alcohol called it, and profit from it. He supported Hinky Dink and Bathhouse in exchange for freedom to run a string of brothels with his wife, Victoria Moresco. His legitimate business, Colosimo's Café, was an enormous success. It attracted the rich and famous where they could hobnob with stars like Enrico Caruso, George M. Cohan, and other luminaries who frequented the night spot when they were in town.

Big Jim became enormously successful in prostitution and gaming. He also became an inviting target for Black Handers. Hoping to be bought off with handsome sums, Black Handers terrorized anyone with money, especially successful gangsters like Colosimo. To insure his personal safety, Colosimo brought in Johnny Torrio, an Italian immigrant from Brooklyn. Having been successful both as a Black Hander and one who fought Black Hand crime, Torrio set to work, craftily, to eradicate the problem. He would agree to pay the demands only to turn on the extortionists. He killed some and scared off the others. Colosimo was relieved of a great burden. As the years went on, he spent more time in his café and left to Torrio, his number one assistant, the job of running his prostitution ring and other illegal businesses.

Because Colosimo enjoyed so much success, he was slow to warm to the opportunities for growth that Prohibition presented. Moreover, enamored by the young actress Dale Winters, he divorced Victoria and took Dale as his second wife. In brief, he had all the money he wanted or needed and had the woman of his dreams. He saw no need to go for more.

Johnny Torrio had a different view.[9] Prohibition furnished a golden opportunity. If he couldn't persuade Big Jim to move on it, then Big Jim had to go. Before long, on May 11, 1920, Colosimo was killed. No one knows if his spurned ex-wife/madam Victoria or Torrio ordered the hit. There was also a third possibility, focusing on political intrigue and rival Italian gangs looking to get a piece of the action, which Kenna and Colosimo had monopolized for so many years. No matter, the end result was an opening for Torrio, who exploited it to the fullest. He developed his own organization. Before he could do so, however, he had to pay his last respects to his fallen leader.

Jim Colosimo's wake and funeral revealed the close relationship, even the friendships, that existed between criminals, businessmen, elected officials, and members of society from all walks of life. At the wake, Coughlin, kneeling at the casket, led hundreds of mourners in reciting Hail Marys.

Later, Coughlin and Kenna led the funeral procession, which included 1,000 members of the First Ward Democratic Club. Over 5,000 people were in attendance, including many from criminal gangs. Johnny Torrio was there. Judges, aldermen, a congressman, and a state representative were among the honorary pallbearers alongside gamblers and saloon owners. It was clear that in Jim Colosimo's world there was no dividing line between right and wrong. Many decades later, law enforcement officials began to act on the realization that funerals of criminals were no different than any other funeral. Friends and relatives came to pay their last respects. In their fight against organized crime figures, law enforcement, especially the FBI, started to film and tape those in attendance. When word of this became known, gangster funerals became, strictly speaking, family affairs. Change also came in other ways. Whereas friendship had been the key element in forging relations between the under and upper worlds, money soon replaced the personal touch in binding them together.

Johnny Torrio quickly established himself as a powerful player in Chicago. Torrio came from Italy to the United States with his parents at age two in 1884. Raised on the lower East Side of New York, he gravitated to the notorious Five Points Gang and headed up the affiliated James Street Gang at an early age. Despite his small stature, he developed a reputation for toughness and was employed by gangsters who were prey to extortionists. It was probably this talent that led his "uncle," Big Jim Colosimo, to call him to Chicago to ward off the numerous Black Handers seeking easy money from their wealthy countrymen. Torrio fit in well with Chicago's master pimp. Having worked in bars and brothels in New York, Torrio was at home running his cousin's brothels, even upgrading them to add a touch of class to an otherwise seedy business. Considered one of the smartest criminals in American history, Torrio saw the benefit of eschewing violence in favor of cooperation and sharing profits with rivals, politicians, law enforcement officers, and members of the bench. He quickly moved to unite the various gangs of Chicago, offering them protection and shared profits in exchange for his leadership. Though it rankled some, particularly Irish gang leaders whose hatred toward Italians was common in those days, Torrio enjoyed much success in the early 1920s. Chicago was a relatively peaceful community. Cooperation was achieved not only on the alcohol front, but in gambling as well.

In 1921, Torrio brought in Al Capone, whom he had known in Brooklyn. Capone served as a bodyguard. Exhibiting loyalty and a deft business sense, he moved swiftly up the ladder and became Torrio's second-in-command. From 1922 to 1924 Torrio made a concerted and successful effort to spread illegal gambling in the Chicago area in partnership with

Capone and Dion O'Banion, one of Chicago's most feared criminals. Together, they owned the Ship, a popular casino in the Windy City. But the tranquillity began to unravel with the coming to power of a reform mayor and the consequent inability of Torrio to provide the degree of protection he had been able to insure with a cooperative city administration. Reform brought with it unintended consequences. Before long, chaos ruled the days. Chicago would earn a reputation for violence and corruption virtually unrivaled in the nation.

When Prohibition became effective, some brewery owners decided to stay in business and have gangsters front for them. A majority of owners opted to sell out. Most of them sold to gangsters. Economists tell us that they were normal people who made rational decisions to go into illegal business. The explanation is in the economists' use of the term *opportunity cost*, which refers to "whatever it is that must be sacrificed to acquire something else."[10] Criminals calculate what they can make legally versus what they can make illegally. They weigh the possibility of being arrested, tried, convicted, and imprisoned. They know that at each step, the chance of getting off is good. Fewer people are tried than arrested. Fewer still are convicted if tried. And finally, not all those convicted are imprisoned. Still, criminals figure what the future costs of imprisonment will be if caught. The gangsters who sold liquor in the 1920s anticipated enormous profits. They figured the money made, often netting millions of dollars annually, would more than compensate for any stretch of time they would have to do if caught. Given the popular climate favoring the repeal of Prohibition in many urban areas where many public officials willingly looked the other way, lawbreakers believed that the chances of not being apprehended to start with were in their favor. Torrio's plan was to bring these disparate groups together and operate peacefully and illegally.

A number of gangs were involved in Torrio's plan.[11] The major ones included the Terry Druggan–Frankie Lake combo, which controlled part of the inner West Side. They were connected with Joseph Stenson, one of Chicago's leading legal brewers before Prohibition who opted to throw in with Johnny Torrio. Rich and respected, Stenson continued to operate, producing near beer and real beer for Torrio, who together became known as the "two kings of crime."

The "Polack Joe" Saltis–Frankie McErlane outfit was active on Chicago's South Side along with the O'Donnell gang. Friction between these two groups, the former pro-Torrio, the latter weakly tied into the plan, would eventually lead to the beer wars that turned Chicago into a shooting gallery. The O'Donnells included brothers Edward "Spike," Steve, Walter, and Tommy. Things went well until Spike was released from Joliet Penitentiary in the summer of 1923. Spike had plenty of clout. In prison for robbery, his parole was supported by a bevy of state senators, state representatives, and a Cook County Criminal Court judge. His old friend, Governor Len Small, happily signed his release papers. Out on parole, Spike was unable to accept the new way of doing business and the Italian leadership that was behind it. Wanting independence, he began moving in on Torrio's territory, hijacking Torrio's beer trucks, breaking up some of his speakeasies, and strong-arming bar owners to handle his product rather than that of Torrio, Saltis, and McErlane. In retaliation, at Torrio's behest, Saltis and McErlane (who introduced the Thompson submachine gun to the underworld) killed many of the O'Donnells' force. Wounded by a spray of bullets from McErlane's machine gun, Spike was so shaken that he quit the rackets.

Torrio's plan of peaceful coexistence with other gangsters was beginning to come apart. It was made more precarious with the election of reform mayor William E. Dever in 1923. Under his predecessor, William Hale Thompson, the underworld had a willing partner in making Chicago a wide-open city. The authorities protected the gangs under Torrio's control. This enabled gangsters to get their share of the profits and remain relatively free from prosecution. They had the best of both worlds. With the coming of Dever, who was unwilling to partner with the bootleggers, producers, and distributors of illegal alcohol, Torrio lost his ability to protect those engaged in illegal activities. His main source of control over potential rivals was lost.

On the West Side was another O'Donnell gang, no relation to the South Side group. Here, William "Klondike," Bernard, and Myles O'Donnell led an all-Irish mob. When Torrio took over Cicero to avoid pressure from Mayor Dever, he offered the O'Donnells a share of the spoils in exchange for their support. They agreed. They were to keep their operations with their own beer and booze, but all other joints in the area would belong to Torrio and company. In the event of trouble, the O'Donnells would provide muscle, as needed, to the Torrio combine. This worked well for Torrio in the early 1920s, but things would change after Torrio retired and Capone took over.

The Genna Brothers (Angelo, Antonio, Mike, Pete, Sam, and Vincenzo "Jim") operated out of Little Italy on the near West Side of Chicago. They hailed from Marsala, Sicily, and had an all-Sicilian clan. Like many Italians in those days, they were slow to accept anyone not from their hometown. Experienced with Black Hand activities and prostitution, the six brothers turned to making alcohol in the 1920s. Employing Italians in their neighborhood, they built a multi-million dollar business. Their product was of the rotgut variety, often bordering on the poisonous, a potent danger to all who consumed it. Their major customer was the Torrio-Capone combo, whom they eventually tried to move in on. That, and accepting two newcomers who were from Marsala, John Scalise and Albert Anselmi, proved to be fatal mistakes. But while Torrio was in command they could still be counted on to support his gang rather than the O'Banions.

It was the Dion O'Banion gang, on the North Side, that was the biggest obstacle to realizing Torrio's plan for sharing peacefully the incredible profits he envisioned. Early on, O'Banion gained experience as a brawler in Chicago's newspaper wars over newsstands and turf. He was ideally suited for any similar battles over booze should they materialize. A former altar boy, O'Banion was a devout Roman Catholic whose flower shop was located across from Holy Name Cathedral. His artful floral pieces were the choice memorials for many deceased, especially victims of gangland warfare. Few who saw him at work daily in his shop would suspect that such a genteel, devoted family man who attended daily Mass could be an impetuous hood who carried three pistols with him at all times and was involved frequently in murder and mayhem. He avoided alcoholic drinks, yet supplied the best alcohol in the city. Nor would he have anything to do with prostitution. During his heyday, not one brothel operated in his North Side area. Still, he thought nothing of shooting people on a whim. Having a cozy relationship with politicians who were indebted to him for his support at the polls, he was right up there with the most feared killers in Chicago. Like his archenemy, Al Capone, he was generous to the needy, especially to anyone he might have injured by mistake.

In pre-Prohibition days, O'Banion had teamed up with Hymie Weiss and George "Bugs" Moran in a string of robberies and burglaries. Both were Catholics. Weiss was Polish and Moran was a combination of Irish and Polish. They were to become deadly enemies of Johnny Torrio and Al Capone. Moran's specialty was his expertise in importing whiskey from Canada. Well dressed and well read, Weiss was renowned for his craftiness and nerves of steel. Often acting as a check on O'Banion's rashness and wild temper, Weiss, when necessary, became a cold-blooded killer. An inventive mind led him to come up with the "one-way ride," which eventually became the method of choice when organized crime hoods decided that someone had to be eliminated. Essentially, this was a way of eliminating a rival in the crime business. The victim would be lured into an automobile on the pretense of discussing a potential mutually lucrative business deal. Once in the car, he would be driven to a remote area, shot, and dumped into some deserted spot. Subsequent hit men would often strangle their prey, attacking from the backseat while the unsuspecting quarry sat next to the driver up front. Weiss was also known to carry rosary beads, which he fingered at times of great stress. Further demonstrating the complicated nature of some of Prohibition's leading criminals was his switch from womanizer to devoted one-woman man. His paramour, lauding their idyllic relationship, said people could easily have mistaken him for a lawyer or a college professor.

The O'Banions had agreed to stay in their territory on the North Side, but were upset when their close friends, the South Side O'Donnell gang, rebelling against Torrio's plan, began to be eliminated by Saltis-McErlane in 1923–24. Though Weiss and O'Banion believed Al Capone to be behind the Saltis-McErlane campaign, Torrio, as leader of the gang, could not be absolved. It was O'Banion's trickery that eventually brought on Torrio's decision to leave Chicago and turn it over to his number one man, Al Capone.

The O'Banions, though agreeing to remain in their North Side territory, often ventured outside it, hijacking Torrio's high-quality Canadian liquor supplied by the Purple Gang from Detroit. They even invaded Torrio's new area of operations in Cicero, which he set up to insure ongoing operations when Mayor Dever made things difficult for his Chicago operations. Despite Capone's advice to use force, Torrio tried in vain to work things out with the O'Banions via compromise. In over a dozen meetings, the O'Banions agreed to respect Torrio's territory, and then proceeded to violate the agreements with impunity. Capone became enraged. He wanted to kill O'Banion. Still, Torrio refused. Peaceful coexistence was his goal. Arbitration was the method to it.

O'Banion continued to insult and assault the Torrio forces. His hatred for Italians and Sicilians came out in his use of ethnic expletives. *Spaghetti-benders* was a favorite of his. Angelo Genna liked to gamble and usually lost heavily at the Ship. Torrio was slow in asking him to pay off his markers, so O'Banion told Genna to pay up or else. The Genna brothers became infuriated and wanted O'Banion dead. At about that time, several of Capone's gunmen were killed. It looked like all-out war would soon erupt. Then, in May 1924, O'Banion seemingly had a change of heart. O'Banion had a controlling interest in Chicago's best brewery, Sieben's. Claiming he had had enough of the constant struggles, he expressed a desire to retire. He offered to sell to Torrio not only his share in Sieben's, but also his share of his gambling interest in the Ship. Torrio felt vindicated. His way had finally prevailed. Peaceful means won out over deadly warfare. He gave O'Banion over half a million dollars in cash. An appointment was set up for May 19, 1924, at Sieben's. Torrio met there with O'Banion and Weiss only to be confronted by over twenty of Chicago's finest. Torrio knew he had been set up. He needed no one to tell him now. O'Banion had to be eliminated.

Torrio knew that getting rid of O'Banion would not be easy. The Irishman was always armed and alert to any possible attempt to assassinate him. He knew most of Torrio's men, certainly the most dangerous ones. The crafty Torrio, once again, called on Frankie Yale, who, one theory had it, was the principal gunman who murdered Colosimo. He came from New York with Albert Anselmi and John Scalise. What transpired next is generally accepted as authoritative; only the principals responsible for the deed differed depending on who told the story.

Mike Merlo, president of the *Unione Siciliana*, a multipurpose mutual benefit society in Chicago, died of cancer. A prominent Italian American well connected to mobsters in the community, his funeral would generate tens of thousands of dollars in flowers, most of it going to O'Banion, who was the unofficial florist for gangster funerals. It was common knowledge that when someone of stature passed away, an informal truce would be observed until the wake and burial took place. In such times, O'Banion would let his guard down. On the eve of his death, Frankie Yale or John Scalise called in an order to O'Banion for flowers for Merlo's wake and said he would be in the next morning with some friends from out of town to pick it up. When three strangers appeared near noon on the following day, O'Banion, assuming they came to pick up the Merlo order, extended his hand to greet them, as was his custom. The three men moved to shake his hand. One of them held on firmly while the others drew their weapons and shot O'Banion dead on the spot. Hymie Weiss swore revenge.

Before long, Torrio was ambushed outside his house. Hospitalized in critical condition, a squad of Capone's men protected him lest Weiss should try to finish the job in the hospital. Recovering in the hospital gave Torrio plenty of time to think about the future. He still believed that a business model could be applied successfully in organizing crime on a peaceful and cooperative basis. His was an early version of the modern franchise operation,[12] which has been effective in selling and servicing products nationally from automobiles to fast foods to Zip packs for computers. But he concluded that Chicago was not ready for such an orderly system. It was not the place for him. Turning over the operation to Capone after taking a generous multi-million dollar "retirement" parachute, he left Chicago. After an extended vacation in Italy, he returned to New York, where his ideas for the development of organized crime were more appreciated. He pursued legitimate real estate interests in Cincinnati, Ohio, and in Brooklyn, New York, where he served as a "consultant" for the mob, whose members held him in high esteem and gave him the nickname "The Fox." He lived to see the heyday of Italians in organized crime, much as he envisioned it, before dying in April 1957 with his wife, Anna, at his bedside. He outlived his star pupil, Al Capone, by 10 years.

It is possible and highly probable that Capone was ecstatic about Torrio's decision to leave Chicago. The fact that Capone was Torrio's devoted pupil does not weigh heavily against that supposition. In fact, it might support it. After all, we are not talking about a legitimate professional and his or her protege. Torrio and Capone were gangsters. Gangsters prized family, friendship, and loyalty. But, above all, they went by the code of business-is-business. Many believed that Torrio was responsible for the death of his "uncle"/mentor Big Jim Colosimo, who was not interested in pursuing the plentiful profits that Prohibition offered. Torrio's leaving willingly avoided the possibility that one day, ambitious to become the crime king, Capone might have to eliminate Torrio. Some thought the Big Fellow eased out Torrio by being behind some of the attempts on his life. That would entail collusion with Hymie Weiss, who hated Capone. Although that is unlikely, Lucky Luciano believed that Capone was behind the hit attempt, though he wept openly when he learned of it.[13] As the years went on, more than a few gang leaders attained their positions by eliminating their bosses. In the early 1930s, as previously mentioned, Lucky Luciano, with help from his Jewish sidekicks, Meyer Lansky and Bugsy Siegel, did away with his two mentors in crime, Joe "The Boss" Masseria and Salvatore Maranzano. In recent times, John Gotti was said to have his soldiers murder Paul Castellano so that Gotti could take over his crime family. Gotti's right hand man, Salvatore "Sammy the Bull" Gravano saved his own skin by turning on his best friend and boss in court. Gravano's testimony was instrumental in putting Gotti away in federal prison, where he succumbed to cancer in June 2002.

Torrio's departure ushered in a new ugly, violent chapter in Chicago's history. Al Capone would play a central role in that sordid, bloody tale.

NOTES

1. See Luciano J. Iorizzo and Salvatore Mondello, *The Italian Americans*, rev. ed. (Boston, 1980), p. 137.

2. Herbert Asbury has a number of books dealing with urban crime. See, in particular, *The French Quarter: An Informal History of the New Orleans Underworld* (New York, 1936); *The Gangs of New York* (New York, 1928); and *The Barbary Coast* (New York, 1933).

3. The Morrissey story is detailed in Virgil W. Peterson, *The Mob: 200 Years of Organized Crime in New York* (Ottowa, Ill., 1983), pp. 35–95 passim; see also the entry in *Biographical Directory of the United States Congress 1774–1989*, Bicentennial ed. (Washington, D.C.: G.P.O. 1989), p. 1539. *New York Times*, 3 May 1878 has Morrissey's obituary. The *Dictionary of American Biography* (New York, 1934), vol. 7, pp. 233–34, contains a two column entry on Morrissey.

4. Becker's tale is told in detail in Peterson, *The Mob*, pp. 116–21.

5. David R. Johnson, *American Law Enforcement: A History* (St. Louis, 1981). See also Ovid Demaris, *Captive City: Chicago in Chains* (New York, 1969); Virgil W. Peterson, *Barbarians in Our Midst: A History of Chicago Crime and Politics* (Boston, 1952).

6. Henry D. Spalding, *Joys of Italian Humor* (New York, 1997), p. 253.

7. Humbert S. Nelli, *The Italians in Chicago, 1880–1930: A Study in Ethnic Mobility* (New York, 1970), p. 149. See also his *The Business of Crime: Italians and Syndicate Crime in the United States* (New York, 1976). Both books have solid material on Colosimo and many Italian American gangsters.

8. See Luciano J. Iorizzo, *Italian Immigration and the Impact of the Padrone System* (New York, 1980), especially pp. 161–209.

9. Torrio is treated in many sources, but see John J. McPhaul, *Johnny Torrio, First of the Gang Lords* (New Rochelle, 1970); a number of sites on Torrio are available at www.crimemagazine.com/torrio.

10. Richard F. Sullivan, "The Economics of Crime: An Introduction to the Literature," in *An Economic Analysis of Crime: Selected Readings*, by Lawrence J. Kaplan and Dennis Kessler (Springfield, Ill., 1976), pp. 15–27.

11. See Jay Robert Nash, *Bloodletters and Badmen: A Narrative Encyclopedia of American Criminals from the Pilgrims to the Present* (New York, 1973), pp. 554–61.

12. The author is indebted to Dr. Joel Swerdlow for noting the similarities in the business models of organized crime and modern franchise operations.

13. Martin A. Gosch and Richard Hammer, *The Last Testament of Lucky Luciano* (Boston, 1974), p. 81.

Chapter 3

CAPONE: THE EARLY YEARS

Al Capone was born in 1899 in Brooklyn, New York, to Gabriele and Teresa Capone. They had come in 1894, taken a house on Navy Street, and later moved to a four-room flat on Park Avenue adjacent to the Brooklyn Navy Yard. Unlike the prestigious Park Avenue of Manhattan, this area was a ghetto home for many immigrants. The Capones brought with them two sons: Vincenzo (b. 1892), later known as Richard James "Two Gun" Hart, and Raffaele (Ralph "Bottles," b. 1894). Salvatore (Frank, b. 1895), the first born in America, had been conceived in Italy. Taking time to acclimate themselves to their new surroundings, it would be four more years before Gabriele and Teresa would have another child, followed by five others. Alphonse (Al), was the second child born in the States. Then Teresa delivered Erminio (John or Mimi, b. 1901), Umberto (Albert, b. 1906), Amedeo (Matthew N., b. 1908), Rose (b. and d., 1910), and finally Mafalda (b. 1912).[1]

Gabriele was a barber looking for a fresh start in life and, unlike Teresa, became comfortable with the new language in America. Still a city then, Brooklyn was connected to nearby Manhattan by two bridges close to Capone's house that spanned the East River, the Brooklyn Bridge and the Manhattan Bridge. Thus easy access was to be had by anyone in Brooklyn with a disposition to join up with the popular gangs of the time that operated in the lower East Side of New York. The Manhattan Bridge took one directly into Little Italy, where many in the Italian American underworld got their start. This hardly seemed to matter for the Capones. Like most immigrants, they were a hardworking family, law-abiding, and striving to fit into their new society. It wasn't always easy. There were formidable barriers. Their broken English identified them as outsiders. Their religion (Roman Catholicism) was not in the mainstream. Their origins as Southern Europeans separated them from the Northern and Western Europeans, who were just beginning to find general acceptance after going through a difficult period of assimilation and acculturation. This was a period in the nation's history when diversity was little thought of save as a negative. Immigrants, though badly needed to fire up the economy, especially as day laborers and agricultural seasonal migrants, were thought of by many as an embarrassment. They were cited as the cause of high crime rates; as the source of economic instability, especially unemployment and labor unrest; and as Europe's throwaways, who were serving to dilute the "racial purity" of America.[2]

Life around the Brooklyn Navy Yard and its docks was often rough-and-tumble. By age 10, young Al Capone had begun to exhibit a toughness and rashness that he carried into his adult life. At 14, he formed the Navy Street Gang to put an end to harassment of Italian women and girls by their Irish neighbors. By then his public schooling was coming to an end. Having done well until the sixth grade, he encountered disciplinary problems that led to a thrashing from the principal. Thus ended his formal education. He had reached the age when many students dropped out to go to work and help support their families, and Capone followed suit.

Just prior to the outbreak of World War I, the Capones moved to Garfield Place. It was an upwardly mobile move that opened up new vistas for the family. Garfield Place was a short street, running uphill from Fourth Avenue, the Italian section, to Ninth Avenue, called Prospect Park West, where it met the park. Though the Capones had definitely improved their lot, it was still a far cry from what lay just a few short blocks away. The farther up the hill one progressed, the higher the social strata, which included some of the richest and most powerful people in Brooklyn. While the Irish had been considered, in the nineteenth century, in a class below that of slaves, their descendants increasingly won favor with the larger American society. By 1900, St. Patrick's Day, once strictly an Irish holiday in America, had become a community-wide celebration. Those who were upwardly mobile were tabbed "Lace Curtain Irish" by those who still struggled economically, the "Shanty Irish." Park Slope had its successful Irish who could be found among the many professionals, businessmen, politicians, and white-collar types living there. George C. Tilyou, the millionaire founder of famed Steeplechase Park, was probably the most famous among them. He had been born in New York City in 1862 of Huguenot/Irish parents. His mother was a Mahoney, and he married Mary O'Donnell in 1893. They had five children whom they raised in their house across from the park, the most exclusive part of the neighborhood. The Tilyous were parishioners and longtime benefactors of St. Francis Xavier Roman Catholic Church, which was down the hill and within walking distance of their residence. Having more Irish parishioners than any other ethnic group, it was one of two magnificent Gothic structures on the block, the other being a Protestant Episcopal edifice closer to the park. The neighborhood was marked by handsome tenement houses that gave way to brownstone homes immaculately kept amidst tree-lined streets the farther up the slope one traveled. Italian boys often pined for the fairer-skinned, lighter-haired beauties, daughters of the well-off, even rich, Irish and White Anglo-Saxon Protestants (WASPs). Rather unrealistically, many young Italian Americans dreamed of dating them, even marrying them. Italians intermarrying with WASPs was virtually unheard of in those days.

Only less unlikely was an Italian-Irish pairing, even though they were often of the same religion. In time, Irish and Italian intermarriages would become common, but they seldom took place in the early twentieth century. Long the whipping boy of the WASPs in the mid-nineteenth century, the Irish were loath to jeopardize their newly won acceptance into the mainstream of American society by associating with the Italians. The Irish relished the opportunity to protect their turf. Catholic bishops and clergy were overwhelmingly Irish. They ran the Catholic church and often relegated Italians to second-class citizenship within it. Some visiting Italian priests were often allowed to say Mass but not given the opportunity to deliver homilies. One altar boy who served Mass for a visiting Italian clergyman wondered if he were somewhat slow since he seldom spoke to anyone. Not until years later did the young altar server realize that the priest was indeed a very bright individual, reigned in because of his ethnicity. The Irish also dominated civil service jobs, the police, the fire department, the docks, and many of the trades. They were not about to let anyone lessen their grip on these areas, least of all the Italians who, by now, were coming to America in droves. It was not until after World War I that the first Italians, led by professionals and general contractors, were able to move into the upper-middle-class neighborhood of what is aptly named Park Slope.

If the Capones could not move into the "forbidden" area on the slope, they could pass through it on their way to the park. Prospect Park afforded citizens a wonderful opportunity to enjoy the simple pleasures of life. People walked there, had family outings, played baseball or football in season, rented rowboats or paddleboats, skied, ice-skated or went sledding, and visited the zoo on the far side of the park. They could even take a short-cut through the park and walk to Ebbets Field to see a ball game when the Brooklyn Dodgers were at home. When Italians wanted to avail themselves of those recreational attractions, the most direct way was to walk up the hill through the Park Slope section. Exposed to this area, many Italians aspired to a better life. Most families who worked at upward mobility did so by getting a good education and working hard. They would grind it out over a generation or two. Those unwilling to wait turned to crime to find quick avenues to success. They knew that once you had money in America, after a while it mattered little from whence it came. The esteem in which descendants of the Robber Barons of the nineteenth century were held was ample testimony to that fact. The example of the Rockefeller family illustrates that. Contemporaries of John D. Rockefeller, the founder of the Standard Oil Company, put him in a class of businessmen and industrialists whom they characterized as ruthless and unscrupulous entrepreneurs who sought monopolistic economic power. They were seen as destructive agents in society. Revisionist historians eventually portrayed them in a positive vein as they pointed to their creative contributions, which led to a more benign growth of America's economic and social welfare. Rockefeller established the Rockefeller Foundation in 1913 to improve the lot of people throughout the world, and his progeny have been widely applauded in their roles as philanthropists, business tycoons, bankers, and politicians.[3]

Closer, more meaningful relationships could be had with non-Italians in areas to the west, away from the park. Gowanus and Red Hook were working-class neighborhoods of Irish and Italians, more in tune with the everyday life of the Italian immigrants. Capone was eventually to meet Mary (Mae) Coughlin in a social club in the Gowanus section on Carroll Street, in what today is called Carroll Gardens. They would marry on December 30, 1918, three weeks after the birth of their child, Albert Francis, known as Sonny. Al was 19; Mae was 21.[4]

At that time, Al's future was uncertain. As a grade school dropout and a teenager, he learned how to use a knife and gun, the latter of which he fired in the basement of the Adonis Social Club (Joe Adonis would later become an organized crime leader, a peer of Lucky Luciano). He joined a gang whose lineage traced back to the Five Points Gang in Manhattan. Its members included Paul Kelly (Paolo Vaccarelli), Johnny Torrio, and the Sicilians Lucky Luciano and Frankie Yale. Torrio and Yale eventually concentrated their operations on Brooklyn. Torrio had set up an office on Fourth Avenue and Union Street, in the heart of Capone's Italian neighborhood. But he moved to Chicago in 1909, when Capone was barely 10 years old. In time, Torrio would have a major impact on Capone's career. For now, it was left to Frankie Yale (born Francesco Ioele) to mold the raw talent exhibited by the youngster. By age 16, Capone was a big, brutish brawler who could knock out an adversary cold with one punch. But using brawn without brains would only lead to unnecessary trouble and draw the unwanted attention of law enforcement. Capone had to be brought along carefully. Yale ran the Harvard Inn in Coney Island. It was a tough joint, a combination bar/brothel where fights often led to killings. Capone worked for Yale as a collector to insure payments from deadbeats, and as a pimp to see to it that the working girls did not withhold part of their proceeds. He then moved to be main bouncer and bartender at the inn. One night he insulted a patron's sister. The customer carved him with a bottle opener (as many old-timers in the Garfield neighborhood remember it) and left Capone with the three gouges by which he would be known the rest of his life: "Scarface." Normally, such an attack would not go unanswered. But the patron was connected to a crime family. Yale convinced Capone that he had violated an unwritten rule of disrespecting a member's family and he would be better off to let it pass. That he did so was a sign that he was smart enough to recognize that it was not wise to go against the higher-ups. Moreover, the fact that he often used the wronged individual as a bodyguard when visiting from Chicago in later years suggests that his respect for family values, on which he prided himself, went beyond his personal relatives.

When Capone married, he seemed to change direction. Before he got into gangs in a serious way, he had worked at legitimate jobs in factories, dutifully turning over his pay of three dollars a week to his mother. That was the expected behavior in Italian homes in those days. Now, married, he would try to return to a respectable life, worthy of his wife. Capone quit working for Yale. Eager to avoid the temptations of his old neighborhood, the gangs, the rackets, and all that this demanded, he moved to Baltimore and took a job as a bookkeeper, which enabled him to hone his skills at accounting, which would serve him well when he began to juggle millions of dollars during Prohibition. Then, abruptly, on November 14, 1920, Gabriele, his father, died of a heart attack. Capone would return to Brooklyn for the services. His flirtation with respectability was over.

Six months prior to Gabriele's death, on May 11, 1920, Big Jim Colosimo had been killed. Though some say that Capone was the hired killer, this is unlikely. Capone was working at that time at a respectable job as a bookkeeper in Baltimore for the Aiello Construction Company. If Torrio ordered the hit, the most likely perpetrator was Frankie Yale, virtually unknown in Chicago and not likely to draw attention to himself. With Colosimo gone, Torrio would need someone he could trust to help him run his bootlegging business as well as the brothels, roadhouses, and gambling casinos. Meanwhile, the Capone family turned to young Al, who had the potential to become the paterfamilias (the head of the household) to whom they could turn for guidance and financial support in times of need.

Capone was at a crossroads in life. He had gained a reputation as a loose cannon, a young man quick to resort to force to settle disputes and who thought nothing of administering brutal beatings. Worse yet, he was suspected of murdering a prostitute (whom he had decided was withholding money from her pimp) and of killing a friend who reneged on a gambling debt to Frankie Yale. He was getting too hot for his fellow gangsters. Two of them advised him to get out of town. Independently of each other, both Yale and Lucky Luciano recommended him to Torrio. Luciano remembered that, when he found out the law was going to come down hard on Capone, he called him to a meeting. When Capone asked what was happening, Luciano said, "I'll tell you what's goin' on; you gotta get the hell outa town and don't bother to pack." With that, Luciano gave Capone $2,000 and told him to go right to Grand Central Station and head for Chicago.[5] Capone saw the handwriting on the wall. He decided to accept Johnny Torrio's offer to join him in his Midwest operations. Eventually, the whole Capone clan would relocate there in the hope that Al would be able to find work and provide for them. To his neighbors in Brooklyn, it was good riddance to bad rubbish. Capone was seen as a punk kid whose removal made the neighborhood a better place in which to live. Many in the area continued to view him in that way even after he became America's most successful and notorious bootlegger.[6]

NOTES

1. See the family tree in Laurence Bergreen, *Capone: The Man and the Era* (New York, 1994).

2. Luciano J. Iorizzo and Salvatore Mondello, *The Italian Americans*, rev. ed. (Boston, 1980), especially chapters 1–6.

3. See articles on "Robber Barons" and "Rockefeller Foundation" in *Dictionary of American History*, 3d. ed. (2003), vol. 7, (New York, 2003), pp. 181–82, 186–87.

4. The author was born and raised in Park Slope, two blocks from Capone's house on Garfield Place. For the relationship between the Irish,

the Italians, and the Catholic Church, see Iorizzo and Mondello, *Italian Americans*, rev. ed., pp. 179–92.

5. Martin A. Gosch and Richard Hammer, *The Last Testament of Lucky Luciano* (Boston, 1974), pp. 30–31.

6. Neighborhood talk over the 1930s, 1940s, and 1950s.

Chapter 4

CAPONE IN CHICAGO: THE FORMATIVE YEARS

Capone came to Chicago in 1921, recommended by Frankie Yale and Lucky Luciano, among others. They knew he was tough and smart. They saw potential in him. He was ready, willing, and able to learn. But he often acted too rashly and attracted too much attention. In fact, he had been very close to being arrested in Brooklyn on suspicion of murder. Luciano and Yale figured that Johnny Torrio was just the right person to guide Capone, to show him the importance of using brains rather than brawn to succeed in the rackets. Torrio put him to work in some of his lower-end bagnios, houses of prostitution. Before long Torrio promoted him to head bouncer and bartender at the Four Deuces, which served multiple purposes. It was a four-story building. The first floor contained Torrio's general offices, a saloon, and a café. The second and third floors had gambling. The top floor was a brothel. It was no place for the weak of heart. Countless unsolved murders took place there. Capone did so well that he was made a quarter partner, sharing in the $100,000 annual income for business. He learned how to profit most effectively from prostitution, gambling, and bootlegging. As a cover, he opened a secondhand furniture store next door and carried business cards announcing his occupation as a furniture dealer.[1]

Capone was by Torrio's side when he concentrated his operations in the suburbs as a hedge against reform movements, which would put a damper on their business in the Windy City. Burnham and Cicero were classic examples of how criminals could control cities and their police and politicians. Most important, Capone was indoctrinated into Torrio's grand plan.

Capone was in the right place at the right time. When Torrio took over from Colosimo, the new leader's ambitious plans convinced him that he would need someone he could trust to help him run the business, especially at night, when "The Fox" liked to spend time with his beloved wife, Anna. He had expanded operations to Burnham, about 20 miles southeast of the Loop. He had interests in dance halls; cribs, which were among the lowest forms of brothels; gambling; slot machines; and roulette. Other entertainment was provided by legitimate musicians and singers, especially jazz groups. With the advent of the automobile, roadhouses became popular. These were taverns, inns, or nightclubs situated by the side of the road in the country. In many of them, customers could get a drink and purchase sexual favors from the ladies of the night who worked for the establishment. Even those without cars could get there by taxi. The hack drivers were familiar with the setup and got a cut of the action for the fares they brought to the night spots. Burnham was an ideal site within range of heavily populated cities like Gary, Indiana, where upwards of 100,000 workers in the steel mills and oil refineries looked forward frequently to a night out on the town.[2]

It would be difficult to find a criminal who had more grudging respect from those on the right side of the law than Johnny Torrio. John Landesco, the sociologist, claimed that Torrio was known as a safe and level-headed bootlegger. Elmer Irey, head of the Treasury Department's Intelligence Unit, who was instrumental in bringing Capone to justice on income tax charges, said that Torrio was really the brains behind modern organized crime. Virgil W. Peterson, noted crime author connected with the Chicago Crime Commission, termed Torrio "an organizational genius."[3] His criminal associates thought no less of him. He practiced what he preached. Rackets was business.[4] Keep a low profile. Rely on cooperation rather than violence. To act otherwise was bad for business and attracted too much attention. He also treated his associates generously and fairly. He expanded the gambling and prostitution begun under Colosimo. For years he convened and presided over gangland's important meetings. He had a knack for foreseeing societal trends. He saw Prohibition coming and acted on it before most did. He purchased legal breweries and charted routes from nearby Canada so as to be able to import liquor when Prohibition went into effect. He made sure that local, state, and federal officials got on his payroll. He organized gangs and, for a fee, set up spheres of influence for them, giving them franchises, as it were. In this way, he would guarantee them protection from the authorities and count on the profits each gang made to insure cooperation among them. And he predicted the end of Prohibition long before virtually all the major bootleggers, many of whom thought their jackpot cash flow would never end. He advised the likes of Lucky Luciano to prepare for repeal. Meyer Lansky, Luciano's close friend and equal in crime, agreed with Torrio when other leaders remained incredulous. Eventually Torrio became a respected elder statesman among criminals.

Torrio's expansion beyond Chicago was key to the development of Capone's empire. At the time of Colosimo's death in 1920, Torrio had already begun to expand his operations into the nearby town of Burnham. There, he owned the Burnham Inn and moved into vice and gambling. He also opened a number of brothels in Stickney and Forest Park. In April 1923, William E. Dever was elected mayor of Chicago. Promising to put an end to illegal gambling and Prohibition offenses, he proceeded to disrupt and close many such establishments. Gamblers and bootleggers had to scramble to survive. Torrio chose to move his operations to Cicero, a western suburb with more than 40,000 people, most of whom were descended from Bohemian immigrants and accustomed to drinking beer as part of daily eating habits.

Torrio started by moving a stable of his prostitutes to Cicero in October 1923. It was a master stroke of misdirection, since he already had all the prostitution business he wanted to handle. His real goal was to move into gambling and the bootleg arena. Since Cicero did not allow prostitution, Torrio was certain that his action would trigger a swift reaction. Sure enough, the police and rival racketeers immediately struck back by expelling his working girls. Using diplomacy, he agreed to forego his brothel interests in exchange for the rights to gambling and selling liquor. Agreeing to honor the O'Donnells' territory in Cicero, Torrio gained acceptance by persuading all concerned that they would share in the profits to be made from illegal operations. Soon thereafter, feeling secure in the deals he made, he set sail for Italy with his mother, whom he would resettle in her homeland. Having already become a millionaire, he set up his mother in a fine estate, stashed some money away safely, perhaps in a Swiss bank account or two, and returned to Chicago in time for the upcoming election in Cicero in April 1924.

The essence of Torrio's plan was to make Cicero a wide-open town where his gang could peddle booze and accommodate gamblers. He would still have to look to other communities like Stickney and Forest Park should he want to expand his vice operations. However, the bottom line was that the Torrio-Capone organization emerged triumphant. Controlling the elections was crucial to their owning the town lock, stock, and barrel. Capone, who had brought two of his brothers into the organization with him, would go to any extreme to keep the incumbents in office. The brothers thought nothing of destroying ballots from the opposition's stronghold and replacing them with votes for their candidates. And, when deemed necessary, they terrorized the electorate. Community officials went along with whatever the Capones did to keep them in office. The police, the sheriff, and the state's attorney either went along with them or felt it futile to try to oppose them. Federal agents, who were not paid off and intent on enforcing Prohibition laws, were thwarted by those locals who tipped off the gangsters of impending raids.[5]

While in Italy, Torrio felt comfortable with Capone in charge. Torrio had been grooming Capone for just such a situation and was aware of the support Capone's brothers, Frank and Ralph, would be able to render the organization. Frank and Ralph proved themselves worthy members of the group. Frank fronted for the outfit. Four years older than Al, he was ideally disposed to become another Torrio. He had the look of respectability and the demeanor to go with it. He had leadership written all over him. Ralph, oldest of the three, was content to concentrate on expanding the gang's prostitution interests. Al, bursting with ambition and still relatively unknown, focused his attention on gambling operations, zeroing in on the gaming emporiums, the Ship and the Hawthorne Smoke Shop, and gaining control of Cicero's Hawthorne Race Track.

While Torrio had worked hard behind the scenes to bring the various gangs together in Cicero, serious opposition to the Capones came from the Cicero *Tribune*. Its young crusading journalist, Robert St. John, exposed their growing influence, especially Al's ambitions to become involved in the day-to-day operations of city government. On one occasion, Capone called for paving the streets with cement and upgrading the landfill. In short, he wanted to be the executive and legislator wrapped into one. St. John's fiery prose mobilized the opposition. Encouraged by the election of the reform mayor of Chicago, William E. Dever, the Democrat Party sought to unseat three-term mayor of Cicero Joseph Z. Klenha, who had always had bipartisan support. Torrio had just returned from Italy, so Boss Eddie Vogel approached him and Capone to insure Klenha's reelection. If successful, the Torrio-Capone combine would be granted immunity from prosecution in any business except prostitution.[6] The opposition also had gangsters working on their side, but the sheer numbers of the Torrio-Capone forces made for no contest. Starting on the eve of the election, March 31, 1924, and continuing the next day, the Torrio-Capone gangsters used guns and fists to intimidate voters, escorted them to the ballot box, and watched as they dropped into it their votes for Klenha. The gangsters held captive honest poll watchers and election officials until the polls closed. Some uncooperative and belligerent citizens were shot and killed.

Even a policeman was manhandled by the mob. While this was going on, concerned Cicero citizens called Cook County judge Edmund J. Jarecki for help. He thought he could defuse the issue by sending a number of Chicago's finest to the scene. Authorized to deputize people, he was able to muster about 70 cops, who went to Cicero in plain clothes and unmarked black sedans. For all intents and purposes they looked like any gang of hoodlums coming into a hostile territory. Spotting Frank Capone at noon on election day, they gunned him down and continued to riddle his lifeless corpse with bullets. Their defense was that he was reaching for his weapon. Judge Jarecki and his marauding force, it seemed, had stooped to the level of the common criminal. Jarecki had precipitated an act of police brutality and ferociousness seldom seen anywhere. If Capone needed anything to stir his latent savagery, this was it. It took all of Torrio's persuasive skill to stop Capone from taking bloody revenge.

This was not the only time that "good people," frustrated by their inability to bring criminals to justice, resorted to vigilantism. Agitated by St. John's exposé of brothel life in Cicero, a minister hired an arsonist to torch the cited bordello. In retaliation, Capone gangsters worked over the young editor and sent him to the hospital. Capone paid all expenses and eventually got St. John to leave town by buying out his newspaper.[7]

Judge Jarecki's efforts to allow the electorate to vote under peaceful conditions were in vain. The mayhem didn't stop. It continued until the polls closed. The Torrio-Capone forces prevailed. Klenha was reelected. Vogel kept his promise. Within one month after the election, Torrio and Capone launched their gambling house, the Hawthorne Smoke Shop, alongside the Hawthorne Inn. It netted close to half a million dollars a year in the first few years. Eventually, Cicero had over 150 gambling houses, selling whiskey, wine, and beer to clients 24 hours a day. Most were owned or controlled by Torrio and Capone and most sold Torrio's beer, willingly or otherwise.[8] Yet it was a bitter victory. Al Capone had forgotten Torrio's admonition to stay out of the limelight. It cost him his brother's life. Moreover, the 1924 election in Cicero threw a spotlight on the utter chaos that could come from alliances between politicians and gangsters. The open warfare, the killing, if even accidentally, of innocent bystanders, the utter disregard for law and order were reminiscent of frontier settlements in the old Wild West, where violence was accepted and human life, at times, was valued less than a man's horse.

Torrio preached nonviolence. He would reluctantly turn to brute force when all else failed. But the name Al Capone was destined to become synonymous with brutality. Try as he might to follow his leader's advice, Capone was plagued by mayhem. He was not blameless. He had a temper that he found difficult to control at times. Growing up in a tough neighborhood of Brooklyn, he was combative. Moreover, he was in a business, bootlegging, which lent itself to fierce competition that could easily get out of hand. The major catalyst, however, was ethnic animosity. There was little love lost between the Irish and Italians. A good many of Capone's adversaries were of Irish extraction, which is perhaps ironic since Capone's wife was Irish. They had little respect for Italians in general. In particular, they had contempt for Capone, the "spaghetti-bender," and preferred to wrest control from him, by murdering him if need be, rather than settle differences peacefully. Like the problems in the Middle East today between the Israelis and the Palestinians, lasting peace, unfortunately, seemed unattainable. With Torrio starting to move out of the scene in Chicago and brother Frank gone, his major motivations to use restraint were removed. The murder of Joe Howard is illustrative.

On May 8, 1924, Joe Howard, a small-time thug, roughed up and bloodied Jack Guzik, Al Capone's partner in the prostitution business, for refusing him a loan. Guzik appealed to Capone for help. Capone immediately sought out Howard in a bar and asked him to explain his actions. Calling him a "dago pimp," Howard told him to get lost. Capone shot him dead on the spot in front of witnesses. It has been suggested that the pent-up emotion of losing Frank finally exploded on being called a pimp. It was the one thing with which Capone refused to be associated. Though eyewitnesses could not recall, later on, seeing anything, and the murder remained unsolved, the press convicted Capone of murder and ran his picture. The original story identified him as Al Brown. Subsequent ones used Alphonse Capone. He was beginning to become a public persona.[9]

Two weeks later, on May 19, 1924, Dion O'Banion set up Torrio for a raid when he was to sell the Sieben Brewery to him. Torrio planned revenge, which he extracted five months later, on November 10, 1924, with the slaying of O'Banion. In the same month, Torrio's remaining major obstacle to his total control in Cicero, the gangster Eddie Tancl, was removed. Tancl got into a shootout in his saloon with some of Torrio's associates who complained of being overcharged for food and drinks. It is said that the killers used that as an excuse to do away with the Bohemian Tancl. The prosecution against Torrio's men was unsuccessful.

In January 1925, Weiss and Moran ambushed Torrio, who came within an inch of losing his life. After he recovered, Torrio was fined $5,000 and sentenced to nine months in jail for operating the Sieben Brewery. While incarcerated, Torrio decided that he had had enough of Chicago's madness. By the end of the year, he had turned over the operation of greater Chicago to Capone and was gone.

Torrio's influence on Capone and the development of organized crime cannot be underestimated. In the four years Torrio ruled in Chicago, he laid down a fundamental criminal business plan, elements of which continue to be utilized by organized criminals today. He took over legal breweries, which he operated in early Prohibition days with the cooperation of officials and some brewery owners. He procured sufficient police and political protection for himself and those in his gambling, vice, and bootlegging activities to solidify his role as a leader. He was able to keep together a disparate group of criminals by virtue of his emphasis on profit sharing and orderly settlement of disputes. When those tactics failed, he resorted to force, which was meted out by his own forces in league with police allies. He expanded into many communities so as to protect against any one venue shutting down his operations in a wave of reform. Particularly insightful was his detachment from incriminating himself by avoiding personally committing overtly criminal acts.[10] His ideas of expansion and accommodation were part of the widening fabric of a national crime syndicate, which branched out into various business and union rackets. As testimony to his valuable contributions to the underworld, he was accepted and looked up to by the likes of Lucky Luciano, Meyer Lansky, Frank Costello, and a host of other gangland chieftains who frequently sought his advice and counsel until a heart attack claimed him in 1957 at the age of 76.

NOTES

1. Fred D. Pasley, *Al Capone: The Biography of a Self-Made Man* (1930; reprint, Freeport, N.Y., 1971), pp. 14 ff.

2. John Landesco, *Organized Crime in Chicago*, Illinois Crime Survey, part 3 (1929; reprint, Chicago, 1968), pp. 41, 85, 94.

3. Cited by Allan May, www.crimemagazine.com/torrio. August 15, 2002.

4. Landesco, *Organized Crime*, pp. 85 ff.; Martin A. Gosch and Richard Hammer, *The Last Testament of Lucky Luciano* (Boston, 1974), pp. 81–94; Laurence Bergreen, *Capone: The Man and the Era* (New York, 1994), pp. 37 ff.

5. Landesco, *Organized Crime*, pp. 85–86.

6. John K. Kobler, *Capone: The Life and World of Al Capone* (New York, 1971), p. 116.

7. Bergreen, *Capone: The Man*, pp. 117–24.

8. Kobler, *Capone*, p. 119.

9. Landesco, *Organized Crime*, pp. 93–95; Bergreen, *Capone: The Man*, pp. 98–124.

10. Landesco, *Organized Crime*, pp. 94–95.

Chapter 5

CAPONE TAKES OVER: THE STRUGGLES CONTINUE

Cicero proved to be a gold mine for Capone. Despite the struggle for turf there, it was not the shooting gallery that the media made it out to be. Robert St. John, Capone's most visible critic, claimed that "ninety-nine percent" of the population "never saw a gangster, never heard a shot fired, never had any contact with all this to-do."[1] Rather, the mob used Cicero's government to control the area. Noncompliant merchants were plagued with higher taxes and loss of parking in front of their stores. They quickly got the message and got in line. Cicero, however, was only part of the story. With O'Banion having been eliminated on orders of Torrio in November 1924, Capone was able to move into the North Side of Chicago and solidify himself with the Gennas. But the peace would not last long.

Biographer Fred Pasley stated unequivocally that the Gennas were the deadliest gang Chicago ever knew. Capone had not retaliated against Weiss and Moran for the attack on Torrio because he had to devote all his energies to keeping the Gennas in check. They had decided to go it alone and presented an extremely dangerous threat to Capone's leadership. They operated openly, with ample police protection, even during Dever's reform administration. Policemen were known to ride shotgun for the Gennas' shipments through hostile territory. Not content with their extremely profitable though limited role, the Gennas sought to take over control of the *Unione Siciliana*, after its president, Mike Merlo, died in 1924.[2] The *Unione Siciliana* was originally a Sicilian mutual benefit society/fraternal group that provided a panorama of benefits for its members and their families. Members, paying minimal monthly dues, were qualified for family benefits that included monetary assistance when struck by illness, unemployment, and death. This was crucial aid for immigrants in an age when there was no national government program covering such emergencies. Each good-sized city might have a number of such mutual aid societies based on immigrant origins in Italy. To be a member of the Unione Siciliana, as the name implies, one would have to have come from Sicily. Most such societies were benevolent—that is, not criminal. From time to time, however, the criminal element might assert itself and take over. So it was with the group in Chicago. The Unione helped fight the Black Hand early in the twentieth century. It was aided by the White Hand Society, which was established in 1907 to bring peace to the Italian community and rid it of its criminal reputation. Employing detectives to expose Black Handers and uncover evidence that could be used in their prosecutions, the well intentioned group received backing from many influential quarters. including the Italian ambassador to Washington and the American and Italian press. After some early successes, the White Hand Society's power quickly waned due to factionalism, class jealousy and mistrust, and the belief held by many Italian workers that crime and political corruption were inevitable products of human activity.[3] Eventually, the Unione, with its thousands of members, became an inviting target. Its treasury could be manipulated and its members used as a political bloc to further gangsters' goals. The major players were the Gennas; the Aiello Brothers, who were allied with the O'Banion-Moran forces; and Capone.[4]

Despite paying off police to the tune of $200,000 a year, the Gennas became millionaires as major suppliers of alcohol to the Torrio-Capone outfit, which also supported them in their violent battles with the O'Banions. But, after O'Banion's murder in 1924, seemingly eliminating their major nemesis, the Gennas were emboldened to strike out against Capone and try to take over his empire. That decision, and getting Angelo Genna elected as president of the Unione, proved to be the undoing of the Gennas.

The Gennas picked Albert Anselmi and John Scalise, two of the most feared killers from their hometown of Marsala, Sicily, to murder Capone. Recognizing Capone's power and fearful that such an attempt would lead to their own demise, the Sicilian duo informed Capone of the Gennas' intentions. He persuaded them to turn on the Gennas. They quickly dispatched Angelo, Mike, and Antonio Genna in late spring and early summer of 1925. Peter, Jim, and Sam Genna fled to Sicily. When they returned to Chicago many years later, they ran a legitimate importing store and stayed clear of the rackets.[5]

When "Bloody" Angelo Genna, so named because of all the people he allegedly murdered, died in May 1925, his associate Samuel "Samoots"

Amatuna, another ruthless killer, announced that he was taking over as president of the *Unione Siciliana*. Samoots was a throwback to Colosimo in that he fancied himself a music impresario. Gifted with a fine tenor voice and able to write some violin pieces, he bought a café in which he would entertain the patrons when the feeling hit him. Backed by the remnants of the Genna gang, Amatuna lasted until November 1925. As Amatuna sat in a barber chair getting a shave and a manicure, two assailants came in and shot him to death. Though no one was ever tried for the murder, it was believed that Vincent "Schemer" Drucci and Jim Doherty of the Weiss-Moran gang were the executioners. Many years later, in New York City, a similar but unsuccessful attempt was made on the life of Frank Costello as he was getting his customary shave and haircut at the Waldorf-Astoria.[6]

The way was clear for Capone to move in on the *Unione Siciliana*. His Sicilian friend Antonio Lombardo took over, and relative peace reigned for the next three years. Capone was free to turn his attention to the surviving O'Banions. They had raided Capone sites a number of times, both in Chicago and Cicero. The move against his Hawthorne headquarters was especially terrifying. Using eight touring cars, they first shot blanks to lure the people outside and followed with live ammunition spewing from machine guns, hoping to kill Capone on the spot. The ruse didn't work. Though 1,000 rounds were fired, no one, miraculously, was killed. Capone was certain that Weiss, Moran, and Drucci pulled off this frightful exhibition of brute violence.[7]

Before Capone could deal with Weiss, he had to defend himself against threats from the inside. Myles and Klondike O'Donnell, who had swung back and forth from pro- to anti-Capone alliances, decided this was a good time to move against their ally in Cicero. They underestimated Capone's determination and ability to get what he wanted. If he couldn't persuade rivals to agree on territorial boundaries, then he would seek to control all of Chicago and its environs. On April 27, 1926, Myles O'Donnell was with some hoodlums, William H. McSwiggin (an Assistant State's Attorney for Cook County), and others. They were on their way after having a few drinks in Cicero when bullets from a passing car killed McSwiggin and two members of O'Donnell's gang. O'Donnell himself escaped. Capone quickly disappeared. Later he reappeared with his attorney, Thomas D. Nash, and claimed innocence. Explaining that he was friends with McSwiggin, Capone stated: "Of course, I didn't kill him.... I liked the kid. Only the day before ... he was up to my place and when he went home I gave him a bottle of 'scotch' for his old man. I paid McSwiggin and I paid him plenty, and I got what I was paying for."[8]

Reinforcing his proclaimed innocence, Capone later testified before Federal officials: "Just ten days before he was killed I talked to McSwiggin. There were friends of mine with me. If we had wanted to kill him, we could have done it then and nobody would have known. But we didn't want to; we never wanted to."[9]

The public was shocked when they heard that McSwiggin was consorting with criminals. Legend has it that Capone, when confronted by McSwiggin's father, gave him a pistol and told the man to shoot him if he thought Capone had killed his son.[10]

There were many theories on why McSwiggin was killed. Some thought he was shot in the line of duty, tracking down information to be used in a case he was working on. Others thought he was slain accidentally, as he was thought to be just another gangster in a group of hoodlums. Some said he was mistaken for Hymie Weiss, the mortal enemy of Capone. The theories went on and on. At the nub of them all were the beer wars. Just as Abraham Lincoln had once said that everyone knew that "somehow" slavery was the cause of the Civil War, Chicagoans understood that "somehow" the beer wars were at the root of McSwiggin's death.

Though the murder was never solved, the seven juries that investigated the slaying threw much light on organized crime and its attempts to control elections, public officials, and the courts. And it demonstrated, as did gangster funerals, the closeness and friendships that existed between criminals and those in law enforcement. The incident was a catalyst in marking the public's interest in organized crime. People would ever after be captivated by the interrelationships of gangsters, politicians, and law enforcement personnel. Many would wonder who would be controlling whom. Did the gangsters call the shots? Were they the pawns of the politicians and/or law enforcement officials, or did the politicians lord it over all of them?

Hymie Weiss, considered by many the smartest gangster of them all, was said to be the only man Capone ever feared. The raid on the Hawthorne was proof that Weiss would stop at nothing to avenge O'Banion's death. Capone could ill afford to ignore Weiss, Moran, and company. Still, a peace was possible. Antonio Lombardo acted as a go-between to set up a truce between Capone and Weiss. If Capone would hand over Anselmi and Scalise, the reputed killers of O'Banion, Lombardo reported that Weiss would agree to a lasting peace. Capone refused. Instead, he sent a hit squad to eliminate Weiss. It included Frank Nitti, Anthony Accardo, Frank Diamond, and the two principals involved, Anselmi and Scalise. They rented a place near Weiss's headquarters in Chicago proper. They watched. They waited. Within a week, on October 11, 1926, Weiss was spotted walking to his shop and was gunned down along with one of his three bodyguards. Capone denied any involvement in the butchery. Since he could prove he was in Cicero at the time, the police didn't even bother to question him. But when pressed by reporters in his headquarters at the Hawthorne Hotel, Capone let it be known that Weiss had it coming to him. Capone told reporters: "Torrio and me made Weiss and O'Banion.... When they broke away... [we] had no objections. Then they started to get real nasty, raiding our territory. We sent 'em word to stay in their own back yard, up North. We pleaded with 'em not to start no trouble, we begged them. They busted into our places, wrecking 'em and hijacking our trucks.... they thought they were bigger than we were."[11]

Capone went on to say that he tried to talk some sense into Weiss after Torrio was shot. He sought accommodations with Weiss to share the wealth and create a peaceful environment so all could live without the tension of being under the watchful eyes of bodyguards day and night. His effort went for naught.

After having made the case convincingly that Weiss's belligerent and destructive moves were aimed at him, Capone stated, incredulously, "I'm sorry that Hymie was killed but I didn't have anything to do with it.... Why should I kill Weiss?" Upon learning of Capone's remarks, the chief of detectives tersely stated: "Capone knows why and so does everybody else. He had Hymie killed."[12]

Capone's most feared competitor was gone. He would still have to deal with Moran, Drucci, and some holdovers from the Genna gang, but they were not nearly the impediment to his power that Weiss had been.

In the fall of 1926, Capone had set out to widen the coordination of rum-running activities. The Unione Siciliana gave him a widespread organization from which to operate. By that time, stockpiles of authentic Scotch whiskey and other pre-Prohibition products were running low. Many people thought Capone to be a hero for trying to import the genuine product from England and other nations. He had representatives in Florida and New Orleans who could supply whiskey from Cuba and the Bahamas. He hooked up with Egan's Rats from St. Louis, the Purple Gang in Detroit, Max "Boo Boo" Hoff's group in Philadelphia, and Frankie Yale in New York. When his New York shipments began to be hijacked, he sent an emissary to New York, James De Amato, to find out why. De Amato was killed there on July 7, 1927. Capone figured that Yale had double-crossed him.[13] He would deal with that treachery in due time.

The Southwest Side of Chicago also presented a problem for Capone. In 1923, allied with Torrio and Capone, the Saltis-McErlane gang had played a major role in ridding the area of the Spike O'Donnell gang. By 1926, Saltis had secretly joined forces with Hymie Weiss. Following the Weiss killing, John "Dingbat" O'Berta, a politically connected member of the Saltis group, presided over a gangland meeting held at the Hotel Sherman in Chicago on October 20 of that year. Capone was there with Moran, Drucci, Jake "Greasy Thumb" Guzik, Ralph Sheldon, William Skidmore, Jack Zuta, and a few others. They agreed that they were only hurting themselves by killing each other and that there was plenty of booty to be had by all if only they would let bygones be bygones. They decreed a general amnesty. The peace was all too short. Urged on by Capone, Sheldon had been contending for turf on the Southwest Side of Chicago for years with Saltis. Only two months passed before a member of Ralph Sheldon's gang was killed. This was more than Sheldon could stand. Having already lost two gunners to Saltis early in 1926, Sheldon declared war on him. In March 1927, Sheldon led two of Saltis's top men into a trap and killed them. Frightened, Saltis and McErlane sued for peace, which was granted by Capone in exchange for a bigger cut of their operations. When McErlane quit, and O'Berta was killed in March 1930, Saltis retired to his country estate in a community he named after himself: Saltisville, Wisconsin. Capone now completely controlled the Southwest Side of Chicago.[14]

NOTES

1. Cited in Laurence Bergreen, *Capone: The Man and the Era* (New York, 1994), p. 117.

2. Fred D. Pasley, *Al Capone: The Biography of a Self-Made Man* (1930; reprint, Freeport, N.Y., 1971), pp. 92 ff.

3. Thomas M. Pitkin and Francesco Cordasco, *The Black Hand: A Chapter in Ethnic Crime* (Totowa, N.J., 1977), pp. 80–81.

4. Pasley, *Capone*, pp. 100–112; Jay Robert Nash, *Bloodletters and Badmen: A Narrative Encyclopedia of American Criminals from the Pilgrims to the Present* (New York, 1973), pp. 16–17.

5. John K. Kobler, *Capone: The Life and World of Al Capone* (New York, 1971), pp. 163–64.

6. Pasley, *Capone*, p. 112.

7. Pasley, *Capone*, pp. 100–121.

8. Cited in John Landesco, *Organized Crime in Chicago*, Illinois Crime Survey, part 3 (1929; reprint, Chicago, 1968), p. 11.

9. Ibid., pp. 19–20.
10. Bergreen, *Capone: The Man*, p. 195.
11. Nash, *Badmen*, p. 604.
12. Ibid.
13. Pasley, *Capone*, pp. 241 ff.
14. Nash, *Badmen*, pp. 483–84.

Chapter 6

CAPONE CONSOLIDATES HIS POWER

In April 1927, William H. Thompson, running on a wide-open platform, was elected mayor of Chicago once again. After four years of exile in Cicero, Capone immediately moved back to Chicago and set up headquarters in the Metropole Hotel. Two rival groups remained to block his dominance over the urban gangs. They were the remnants of the O'Banions and the Gennas. For a while, Capone and his rivals worked together. Reverting to the Torrio strategy, the gangs formed a syndicate and shared in the gambling, vice, and booze profits while enjoying protection and immunity from arrest for its members. The owners of the roadhouses, dives, and assorted illegal enterprises had no choice but to pay to insure that neither the mob nor the law would harass them.

The peace was tenuous. Offspring of a mixed ethnic marriage (Polish/Irish), Bugs Moran ran with Irish gangs as a teenager, specialized in robbery, and joined O'Banion's gang in 1910 at the age of 17. By 1927, with Weiss eliminated by the Capone forces and Vincent Drucci killed by a policeman in April 1927, Moran took over. He was as eager to get rid of Capone as Weiss had been. Moran had plenty of guts, but little common sense. He publicly denounced Capone, especially for peddling women and bad alcoholic beverages. Constantly on the attack, Moran's troops launched a number of forays against Capone's businesses.

In January 1929, Moran and Joseph Aiello, who had pulled together the remains of the Gennas, joined forces for an all out assault against Capone. Both sides lost considerable numbers of soldiers as they fought for supremacy of the rackets. Capone himself became the number one target. In fact, from 1925 on, there had been a number of attempts on his life.

Indeed, his life expectancy was so short that no insurance company would issue him a policy. Weiss, Drucci, and Moran all failed in their attempts. Drucci, on one occasion, tried in vain to shotgun Capone to death in Hot Springs, Arkansas, normally considered an open city, a safe city, where criminals could go without fear of ambush. Word on the street had it that Aiello was offering $50,000 to anyone who would murder Capone. In 1927, Aiello imported killers on numerous occasions to take him up on the proposition. Would-be assassins came from New York, St. Louis, Cleveland, and Milwaukee. Capone's network found them out, and the would-be killers wound up dead. Frustrated, Aiello tried to get Capone's private cook to poison his employer. The cook refused and reported Aiello's murderous intentions to Capone. Then, on January 8, 1929, it was said that Aiello and Moran gunned down Pasquilino Lolordo, yet another president of *Unione Siciliana* whom Capone had supported. This was the last straw. Capone's waiting game was over. He went after Moran with a vengeance. He ordered a hit. No ordinary hit. It was to be a multiple murder unleashed with bestial fury. Known as the St. Valentine's Day massacre, it would become infamous around the world.

The St. Valentine's Day killings have been told and retold in gory detail in books, movies, and television shows. The killers, disguised as policemen, entered Moran's warehouse and caught the seven victims off guard. Facing them against the wall as if to frisk them before arresting them, the hit men mowed them down with a barrage of machine gun fire. Moran was not among them. On his way to the warehouse, he beat a hasty retreat when he saw what appeared to be a police raid. The lookouts had mistakenly identified Al Weinshank, a gang member who looked like Moran, from a distance and gave the green light for the attack. No one was ever convicted of the crimes. John Kobler, one of Capone's better biographers, states that the only one who can be said with certainty to have taken part in it is Fred "Killer" Burke, a member of Egan's Rats from St. Louis. Anselmi, Scalise, "Machine Gun" Jack McGurn, George Zeigler, Gus Winkler, "Crane Neck" Nugent, and Claude Maddox, another Missourian, were also thought to be involved in some way.[1]

Prior to that time, Capone was viewed as one of Chicago's most feared criminals, on par with Torrio, O'Banion, Weiss, and the Gennas. By 1928, though, many considered Capone to be "the king of the underworld," but it was noted that he had "not as yet succeeded in securing the position of uncontended supremacy held by Torrio."[2] After St. Valentine's Day, he was counted in a class by himself. Ironically, as he came closer to eliminating all his rivals, his star began to fade. Still, he had unfinished business. Moran had avoided the attack intended for him. Affected by the deaths of his men, he became a non-factor in syndicated crime, turning instead to petty burglaries. Without political clout to protect him, Moran did time for bank robberies in Ohio State Prison and Leavenworth Federal Penitentiary, where he died in 1957. Joseph Aiello continued to be a thorn in Capone's side. Moreover, Capone's loyal supporters, Giuseppe "Hop Toad" Guinta, Albert Anselmi, and John Scalise soon attempted to betray him.

Guinta had taken over as president of the Unione Siciliana with Capone's approval, but, with increasing pressure being put on Capone by the authorities, Guinta thought he could take over his supporter's operation. He persuaded Anselmi and Scalise, vice executives of the Unione, to join him. Their plotting was discovered by Capone's bodyguard, Frankie Rio. On May 7, 1929, Capone threw a gala at the Hawthorne Inn. He invited his top shooters. including the trio that would betray him. After the guests were intoxicated, he proceeded to beat the treacherous trio to death with a baseball bat. Their mutilated bodies, with virtually all their bones broken, were found in their abandoned car across the state line in Indiana. Within three months, two ghastly massacres had occurred. Capone had to lay low. He went to Atlantic City, where gangland leaders from across the country were meeting to discuss the future of organized crime.[3]

In Chicago, only Aiello remained. Capone had thought he eliminated any serious threat from Aiello in 1927. At that time, Capone had arranged to have Aiello brought in for questioning for a murder. Capone, then, managed to place three of his men in a cell next to Aiello. They threatened to kill him. He pleaded for his life. Capone's men told Aiello to leave town and he would be spared. He moved to Trenton, New Jersey. But, in 1929, Aiello found renewed courage and determination to attempt to overthrow Capone. He went so far as to take over the presidency of the Unione Siciliana. Like so many presidents before him who were killed while in office, Aiello's luck soon ran out. On October 23, 1930, he was machine gunned to death. Capone had finally neutralized or done away with all his competitors.[4]

NOTES

1. John K. Kobler, Capone: The Life and World of Al Capone (New York, 1971), pp. 247–61.

2. John Landesco, Organized Crime in Chicago, Illinois Crime Survey, part 3 (1929; reprint, Chicago, 1968), pp. 11, 95.

3. Kobler, Capone, pp. 262–66.

4. Jay Robert Nash, Bloodletters and Badmen: A Narrative Encyclopedia of American Criminals from the Pilgrims to the Present (New York, 1973), pp. 16–17; Kobler, Capone, pp. 232–33.

Chapter 7

ORGANIZING CRIME

Gangsters took a great leap forward in organizing crime from the 1920s on. They began to hold conferences to discuss matters of mutual concern. The first known conference was held in Cleveland, Ohio, in December 1928. The conferees were all Italian, many of whom were the upcoming leaders of organized crime. Fearful of losing some of his power if he attended, Capone stayed away. He sent a representative instead. Though little is known for certain of what went on, the conference set a precedent for gangland meetings and opened the way to the Americanization of "foreign" gangsters. In the Cleveland meeting and subsequent ones, organized criminals followed the example of American businesses in using conventions to bring leaders together to discuss business and exchange ideas. Virtually every profession and industry in America had its annual conferences. Though not meeting yearly, organized crime was no exception. The major difference was that organized criminals did not publicize their get-togethers. No one can say with certainty how many such meetings took place.

The main business item in Cleveland possibly had to do with corn sugar, a necessary item in the production of whiskey. Mob leaders wanted to be sure that its supply and distribution would be constant and orderly so as to maximize their profits. Coming soon after the killings of Frankie Yale (1927) and Tony Lombardo (1928) the convention in all probability dealt with overseeing an orderly transition of leadership in the *Unione Siciliana* in New York and Chicago.[1]

When gangland leaders met again the next year in Atlantic City, Capone was there. He must have figured it was better to keep an eye on what was going on than have racketeers possibly conspiring behind his back. Criminals were taking a big step forward in allocating turf and rackets to major bosses and putting an end to chaos and bitterness. Though there are no minutes of the meeting extant (if there ever were any), various authors have come up with a number of agenda items that were discussed and agreed upon. Who attended and who was not invited speaks volumes about the direction, assimilation, and Americanization of first- and second-generation immigrants in organized crime. Al Capone and Jake "Greasy Thumb" Guzik came from Chicago. King Solomon represented Boston. "Boo Boo" Hoff, Waxey Gordon, and Nig Rosen came from nearby Philadelphia. Moe Dalitz led a contingent from Cleveland that included Lou Rothkopf and Leo Berkowitz, who went by the name of Charles Polizzi. A large delegation headed by Abe Bernstein drove in from Detroit. Boss Tom Pendergast, the Kansas City political leader, named John Lazia as his representative. New York sent more gangsters than any other city: Johnny Torrio, Lucky Luciano, Meyer Lansky, Longie Zwillman, Willie Moretti, Frank Costello, Lepke Buchalter, Joe Adonis, Dutch Schultz, Albert Anastasia, Vince Mangano, and Frank Scalise. With the demise of Abe Rothstein, a major force in modernizing organized crime, in November 1928, Frank Erickson stepped in to lend his expertise in the gambling area.

But the so-called mafiosi, Joe "The Boss" Masseria and Salvatore Maranzano, were not invited. Both were Sicilians and leaders of major Italian gangs in New York City. Bitter enemies, they each aspired to become the "boss of bosses," undisputed head of the five Italian crime families operating in the New York metropolitan area. Luciano had good reason to keep these two *Dons*, a name commonly given to Italian crime bosses, away from the convention. They were not of a mind to open up their operations to non-Italians. They held to their old-world ways of associating only with their own kind, Sicilians. They would have stuck out like sore thumbs amid the multiethnic gathering and probably would have made a smooth-flowing session impossible. Luciano and Lansky were convinced that the wave of the future for their syndicate was to integrate the best mobsters they could find. They were not concerned with ethnic exclusivity or old-world customs and ways of doing business, which they believed to be unproductive in the American setting. They were expansive-minded and felt that the conservative, narrow-minded approach would limit their chances of growing the business. Just the presence of Masseria and Maranzano would push Luciano and Lansky into the background unless they wanted to challenge their leadership openly. They wanted to set the agenda and deal effectively with the business at hand.

The Atlantic City convention nipped in the bud any chance for the flowering of the Mafia in America. Whatever progress (if any) Sicilians had made in transplanting their old-world customs in the United States and whatever hopes they had of infiltrating and influencing the society at large, as had been done in their homeland, was brought to an abrupt halt. The major business accomplished dealt with organization, gambling, and liquor.

The conferees agreed on establishing an organization of equals that would have jurisdiction throughout the nation. There would be no boss of bosses. Murder would be outlawed. Rule would be by a commission that would recognize the sovereignty of leaders on their turf as long as they abided by the rules for the syndicate on which all had agreed. There was plenty of money to be made in providing consumers with liquor, women, and gambling. Everyone stood to profit by agreeing to assigned territories and sticking to their promises.

Illegal gambling was one of their prime concerns. It was central to establishing organized crime on a national level, more so than even Prohibition. There was plenty of room for expansion in gambling. Through the efforts of Al Capone, Moses Annenberg, and Frank Erickson, the mob was able to establish a lay-off betting system throughout the country in conjunction with a national wire for horseplayers and the *Daily Racing Form*, the Bible of the sport of kings. Annenberg had a crucial role to play in attracting horseplayers. He provided the necessary information they needed to handicap the races and formulate their bets. The *Form* furnished information on horses: their past performances, jockeys, trainers, and other vital data. Annenberg also provided scratch sheets which came out close to post time and gave the latest information relative to the day's program, including late scratches and jockey changes. The wire service piped the call of the race into the bookmaker's establishment. In this way, punters (another name for bettors) could go about their business as if they were at the race track, collecting their winnings after a race was run and made official or rationing their stake to last the full racing card if their horses lost. The importance of racing information and the wire service is clear. They made betting on horses attractive. Communities that lacked those services had few, if any, horseplayers. No one wanted to bet on a horse if he or she could not find out if the horse won until the next day or two. Gamblers usually want instant gratification. If one lived in an area that got an early edition of a newspaper, one would have to wait two days for the results of a late-run race. The bettors would soon lose interest in betting on horses.

Rothstein had provided the key to nationalizing gambling, lay-off betting, shortly before he was killed in 1928. In essence, it gave protection to

bookmakers against being wiped out by heavy betting on one horse by allowing them to "lay off" the bet—that is, give a good portion of the action
to another bookie or bookies in an area where there was little support for
the particular horse involved. In effect, they were balancing the books.
This eliminated, or greatly minimized, the gamble for the bookmakers,
and made them businessmen. It guaranteed them a profit by allowing
them to act as their own pari-mutuel machine. That is, the winners would
be paid off with the money from the losers. When the state operates a
pari-mutuel system, it takes off the top what is its due and divides the re-
mainder among the winners. Gamblers/businessmen had to settle for what
was left over after paying the winners. Since bookmakers usually had a
limit on their payouts as a protection against long shots winning, their
gross was usually enough to pay for expenses and furnish a comfortable net
profit. In time, the lay-off system could be utilized for any bet in any sport
where a lopsided betting pattern developed. In this way, organized crime
developed a profitable service for which it extracted a percentage of the
action, commonly called "vigorish" today. More importantly, this innova-
tive device connected gamblers throughout the nation. Since many of
them were also gangsters, the formation of a national crime syndicate was
facilitated. Prohibition had also made it possible for gangs around the
country to centralize. But it only existed for about a dozen years and invited too much treachery and uncooperativeness. Gambling, on the other
hand, has existed from colonial times up to the present. Based on cooperation, it was and continues to be organized crime's least objectionable activity and its most consistent moneymaker.[2]

On the liquor front, the conferees sought to eliminate cutthroat bidding for liquor abroad, thereby causing its price to drop and raising profits
for all concerned. They would prepare for the time when Prohibition
would end by buying breweries, distilleries, and liquor import franchises.

A major problem facing the attendees was what to do with Al Capone.
Capone had attracted a tremendous amount of unwanted attention with
the St. Valentine's Day massacre and the brutal bludgeoning to death of
Giunta, Anselmi, and Scalise. Luciano, Lansky, and others sought to neu-
tralize the "king" of Chicago. Torrio was set up as manager of the new
commission, which would settle all disputes. Joseph Aiello, Capone's old
enemy, would head the *Unione Siciliana* in Chicago. Capone would have
to cede his gambling operations to the commission.

Ironically, Capone, at the height of his career, was being read the riot
act by his own peers. They, not the police or politicians, were his worst
enemies. He knew the agreements were not enforceable. He also knew
that he would probably be eliminated unless he made some concessions.
He decided to buy time. Since so many gangsters around the country

wanted him to lie low for a while, Capone thought it best if he did so. This scenario makes the most sense given what transpired soon after in Philadelphia. Most writers agreed that he arranged for some friendly policemen to arrest him for carrying a gun. Here was a man whom authorities had been trying to jail in vain for years. He had a battery of the best attorneys at his beck and call. But, within 16 hours of leaving the meeting, he started serving a one year jail sentence for carrying a concealed weapon. He was arrested and booked on the night of May 17. The grand jury indicted him at 10:30 A.M. on May 18. He pled guilty at 11:30 A.M. The presiding judge sentenced him at 12:15 P.M., and Capone started serving his sentence at 12:45 P.M. Capone entrusted his size $11^1/_2$ diamond pinkie ring to his attorney with instructions to give it to his brother, Ralph. He would become acting head until Al returned.[3]

Whether or not this was the best way for Al Capone to solve his immediate problem will never be known. Had he returned to Chicago or Miami Beach, where he had recently established residence, he would have continued to be in the limelight no matter how hard he tried to avoid it. He would have been extremely vulnerable to an attempt on his life. Prison kept him under wraps. What is certain, however, is that Capone had reached the height of his power. The events of Atlantic City and Philadelphia dashed any hopes he might have had of extending his kingdom nationally. There was only one way he could go now: down.

Before any meaningful progress could be made on implementing the plans to diversify and expand put forth at Atlantic City, those who opposed the idea, namely Masseria and Maranzano, would have to be dealt with. They had been warring to see which one would become "the boss of bosses" in their limited ethnic world. When Masseria's top lieutenant, Lucky Luciano, saw the tide turning against his patron, he engineered Masseria's killing. Maranzano now proclaimed himself as the sole leader of all the Italian crime families and rewarded Luciano by naming him to supervise the whole underworld operation. Maranzano set up five families in New York and expected to rule for a long time using old-world Mafia methods. Members would be sworn to silence. They must obey without question. They could not use force against one another, nor could they covet another's business or wife. Of course, only Italians could belong to this thing, which Joseph Valachi later described as *La Cosa Nostra*, literally "Our Thing" or "This Thing of Ours." Maranzano didn't last long. Luciano had other ideas and plenty of support within the organization.

Joe Valachi was a lower-level member of the Vito Genevose crime family who was serving time in Atlanta Penitentiary. Thinking that Genevose, who was incarcerated there also, was out to do him in, he bludgeoned to death a prisoner he mistook for the person he believed his former boss had sent to kill him. Looking to save himself from a death sentence, he agreed to cooperate with the FBI and tell the Senator McClellan Investigating Committee all he knew about organized crime. Essentially, he described an organization of 24 crime families based on Italian heritage that he called La Cosa Nostra (LCN) and which virtually everyone in America came to identify as the Mafia. The McClellan Committee concluded in 1963 that LCN was "a private government of organized crime, a government with an annual income of billions—run by a commission [that] makes major policy decisions for the organization, settles disputes among the families and allocates territories of criminal operation within the organizations."[4] Though he never used the word *Mafia*, Valachi made a major contribution to popularizing the myth and mystique of the Mafia in America.

Two months after Masseria's demise on April 15, 1931, Luciano met in Cleveland with Moe Dalitz, Santo Trafficante from Tampa, a representative of Capone, and a few other gangsters eager to rid themselves of the tyrannical leader Maranzano. Getting wind of the meeting and suspecting they were plotting against him, Maranzano marked Luciano, Costello, Adonis, and others for death. Before he could execute his plan, four men posing as federal agents entered his office and knifed and shot him dead.

Not long thereafter, though he was in the midst of the trial that would cost him his freedom, Capone hosted a multiethnic gathering of underworld figures. They had eliminated the leaders, Masseria and Maranzano, who wanted to maintain an all-Sicilian-Italian mob. They could now proceed with the plans first put forth at Atlantic City to develop a national crime syndicate that Arnold Rothstein, New York City's premier gambling boss, and Johnny Torrio had advocated a few years prior.

Those in attendance in Chicago were representative of the increasing cooperativeness of gangsters representing diverse ethnic backgrounds. They applauded Luciano for his role in getting rid of Masseria and Maranzano. He, in turn, convinced the mostly Italians, Irish, Jews, WASPs, Poles, and Scandinavians that their futures would be brighter if there were less intimidation and violence in their dealings. They should all be equals. There would be no boss of bosses. To punctuate his comments, he turned down envelopes filled with cash, which Italians customarily gave to a newly recognized leader. Capone thought that Luciano had needlessly gone too far in breaking with tradition. But, Luciano insisted, it was the best way to show gang members that he was instituting a new order. There would still be a hierarchy, but it was less rigid. He recommended a *consigliere* who would act as an advisor looking out for the best interests of his leader and as an ombudsman—that is, an agent protecting the rights of gang members by ironing out differences in the ranks and between the "soldiers" and their superiors. As a sop to tradition, Luciano went along with calling this new group *Unione Siciliana*. He preferred the "Outfit." Some Italians would use La Cosa Nostra. Other members chose the "Syndicate," or the "Combination."

After World War II, *Mafia* came back in vogue. A number of major players other than Luciano were non-Italians: Lansky, Dalitz, Bugsy Siegel, Abe Reles, and Dutch Schultz. Thus, *organized crime* should have best described this new organization. However, since it was often used as a euphemism for the Mafia, Italian criminals continued to get more than their share of credit for running the rackets.

In sum, a diverse group of gangsters meeting in Chicago established a national organization to bring independent gangs together, help stop internal war among themselves, and rid the group of traditional Sicilian ideas of ethnic dominance. Capone could not be happy with his role, which was largely ceremonial. Still, he found reason to be pleased. Though he had a reputation for spewing fear and violence around Chicago, he had attempted to carry out Torrio's ideas of organization, diversity, and peaceful coexistence among fellow gangsters.

NOTES

1. Humbert S. Nelli, *The Business of Crime: Italians and Syndicate Crime in the United States* (New York, 1976), pp. 213–14.

2. Martin A. Gosch and Richard Hammer, *The Last Testament of Lucky Luciano* (Boston, 1974), pp. 103–8 deals with the Atlantic City conference.

3. Laurence Bergreen, *Capone: The Man and the Era* (New York, 1994), pp. 336–38.

4. Norval Morris and Gordon Hawkins, *The Honest Politicians Guide to Crime Control* (Chicago, 1970), p. 211; Peter Maas, *The Valachi Papers* (New York, 1968), pp. 25–47.

Chapter 8

CAPONE IN FLUX

Scarcely two years after he had taken control of the organization from Torrio, Capone knew he had a big price to pay for being number one. Capone had supported William H. Thompson, who became mayor for the third time. Capone reportedly had given as much as a quarter million dollars to Thompson's campaign. In return, Capone operated gambling halls and booze dens without fear of interference from Chicago's finest. Thompson had previously made it plain that he was no prohibitionist. He said publicly that he was "wetter than the middle of the Atlantic Ocean."[1] But things changed. Thompson wanted to be president of the United States. He knew Capone would be a burden, a symbol of all that was wrong with Chicago. Capone's exploits made for lurid reading even in Europe, where people were titillated by stories of his armored car cruising the city amidst bombings while his bodyguards shot up the streets. Europeans looked upon Chicago as the crime capital of the world. Noting that the police were quick to blame him for any murder that took place in the city, Capone stated at one point: "They've hung everything on me except the Chicago fire."[2] His reputation spread so far and wide that even people from abroad tried to enlist his help in doing away with their rivals. The pressure became unbearable for his wife and mother, who suggested that a move to a more hospitable clime might do them all good.

Capone went to Los Angeles in early December, 1927. Accompanied by his wife, son, and two bodyguards, he registered as "Al Brown" at the Biltmore. Not fooled by the alias, the press exposed him, and the public protested vehemently against his presence. Police Chief James E. Davis declared him persona non grata (unwelcome) and gave him 12 hours to

leave town. Capone protested in vain. Within a few days, he and his entourage started back home. But Chicago's Chief Michael Hughes was ready
for him and gave orders that should Capone show his face in town that he
should be jailed. Capone slipped quietly into town. Having detrained in
Joliet, Illinois, he came by car with his brother Ralph. Determined to fight
for his rights, he told a reporter:

> I'm going back to Chicago.... I've got a right to be there. I
> have property there and a family. They can't throw me
> out...unless they shoot me through the head. I've never done
> anything wrong. Nobody can say I ever did anything wrong.
> They arrest me. They search me. They lock me up. They
> charge me with all the crimes there are, when they get me into
> court. The only charge they can book against me is disorderly
> conduct, and the judge dismisses even that because there isn't
> any evidence to support it.... I've been the goat for a long
> time. It's got to stop some time and it might as well be now. I've
> got my back to the wall. I'm going to fight.[3]

Capone was right. Chief Hughes could not exile him simply based on
his bad reputation. Capone had legal rights. He owned property and paid
local taxes. As a matter of fact, he had taken up permanent residence in
an upscale neighborhood far removed from the rough-and-tumble world
of the notorious sites where he did business. He left behind the gambling
joints, the blind pigs (speakeasies), and alky cookers. He lived among respectable WASPs, who considered him a good neighbor. His wife, mother,
and other members of the Capone family enjoyed the gracious city living
of a quiet middle-class section. Hughes did the next best thing. He ordered the police to put the Capone household under 24-hour surveil-
lance.

As abruptly as Capone fell out of favor with the Thompson regime, he
regained his position of power as strong as ever. When the mayor realized
that no one was taking seriously his run for the presidency, alliances with
the mob were reinstituted. Capone felt like his own self again. Still, he
had to prepare for contingencies. What if the winds of change blew
against him again and jeopardized his standing? He needed a safety net, a
retreat to which he could repair in times of trouble. Scouting a number of
warm-weather communities, none of which appeared to want him, he decided that Miami afforded him the best chance for success in his quest.

South Florida proved to be an ideal location to spend the winter. No
place in the continental United States had the combination of sunshine

and warmth that carried through the night. The breezes off the Gulf Stream were warm enough to fend off most any frost that might threaten from the north. Miami was not tropical, but it was the next best thing to it. People could relax there; be casual in their dress; be active if they desired. They didn't have to fight ice, snow, or blizzards. They didn't have to worry about car troubles due to freezing temperatures, which not only ran down batteries, but also gummed up transmissions. The little and big annoyances of winter living disappeared. All things being equal, it was easier under these circumstances to lead the easy life in sunny South Florida. People of means had discovered Miami and its environs and were taking advantage of its climate, beaches, arts, theatres, and fashionable restaurants. Business magnates would travel to the area with their own railroad cars and spend months at a time resting and recuperating. At the season's end they would return north, feeling fit and looking the part with their bronze glow. It appeared to be just what the doctor ordered. Capone wanted a part of that life. It would not be easy to gain acceptance. People looked on him as a violent man, quick to anger, looking to corrupt society, and likely to soil the reputation of an otherwise decent community, thereby impeding healthy economic and social growth. Women's clubs, churches, and businessmen's organizations saw him as a liability. They vigorously protested his presence. But there was hope. Some of those who opposed him did so for public consumption. They would accept his favors when the right time came along.

Capone persisted. Renting a bungalow for the season under the name of Al Brown, he was able to go about town and make the acquaintance of people who would one day help him to settle there permanently. Parker Henderson Jr., the son of a late mayor of Miami, proved to be especially helpful. He became Capone's key go-between in helping the gangster buy a house on Palm Island, get money from Chicago via Western Union using still another alias, and meet influential people who could persuade Miamians that Capone had no intention of getting into the rackets there, that he would be good for their city.

The opposition to Capone had to be balanced by the sorry state of the economy. Florida, and Miami in particular, were suffering from the busted land boom. Business interests were especially hopeful that an accommodation could be worked out to keep Capone there. He had plenty of money and was eager to spread it around. He talked of opening legitimate businesses, joining the Rotary Club, playing golf and tennis, essentially doing all the things that a typical citizen might do when moving into a new community. He ingratiated himself to the local politicians, all of whom became indebted to him for his financial aid. Equally important, he gave the Miami politicians an out by settling in Miami Beach, a distinct political entity. In reality, there was little difference between the two. They were separated by the intracoastal waterway, over which a bridge provided easy access between Miami on the mainland and the beaches. Vacationers would probably not be able to tell when they were in one or the other because they would always be crossing bridges. South Florida is like that, a land of water and bridges where communities often meld into each other unnoticeably. Thus, officials in Miami could oppose Capone for show, but line up in his presence for dough.

Capone used his villa on Palm Isle to entertain visitors from the north as well as Miamians, many of whom felt a certain rush at being in the company of America's most feared individual. They lounged around. They fished. They enjoyed Capone's huge swimming pool, which was among the first in the area to use filtered water. They took rides on his numerous watercraft, which featured a speedboat and cabin cruiser. Sometimes Capone chartered a seaplane to fly his guests to Bimini or some other island hideaway.

Capone enjoyed life in Miami. Having reveled in the nightlife of Chicago, he found a certain element in the heart of South Florida that exuded excitement and was willing to accept him. The action after dark was captivating and featured some of America's best musicians and entertainers who played the Florida winter circuit. Capone lavishly entertained many of them in his home. There were headliners such as Eddie Cantor, George Jessel, Al Jolson, Joe E. Lewis, and Harry Richman. He often went to the theater and the fights. A horse-racing devotee back home, he found that Hialeah Racetrack, in the afternoon, featured not only the best of the thoroughbreds, but also a romantic setting with its flamingos in flight. Capone also benefited psychologically. Miami and Naples, Italy, had many similarities. He could better appreciate the roots of his parents. Naples had a panoramic view of the bay, its beauty enhanced by the sight of the Isles of Capri and Ischia, world-known for their romantic allure. The two cities had similarities of coastal waters, abundant sunshine, pleasure and fishing boats coming and going, and ocean liners and cargo ships adding to the hustle and bustle. They had a good share of tourists from many nations. Almost a carbon copy of Naples, Miami's scene surely evoked memories in Capone that were instilled in him on his mother's knee. He would stay in Miami.

In 1929 Capone did a stretch in Pennsylvania for carrying a concealed weapon. When he got out the next year, he found a changed atmosphere. In Florida, the anti-Capone crowd had gained in influence. It would not be seduced by his hospitality and friendship. Influential Miamians viewed

Capone's jailing in Pennsylvania as the last straw. Fearful that Capone's return might change Miami into another Chicago, they pressured Florida's governor Doyle E. Carlton to take drastic action. He responded by alerting all the sheriffs in the state. He ordered them to run Capone out of town if he showed up. But Capone was a property owner and taxpayer in Miami Beach. Legally, he had every right to be there. This clearly was an extralegal maneuver on the part of Governor Carlton. Eventually, Capone's attorneys sought and won a permanent federal injunction against the governor's order.

Many Miamians enjoyed the illegal gambling and boozing provided by the locals. Given the absence of violence in dispensing these illicit services, they saw nothing wrong with that or with the people who serviced them. However, the anti-Capone forces took a different view of the Chicagoan. They felt he was not one of their own. They didn't view him as just another "businessman" providing illicit services. He was an outsider, a dago gangster with a reputation for murder and mayhem. These upper crusts of Miami convinced city officials that Capone did not belong in their city. Their constant complaints led to Capone's arrest on four occasions on charges of suspicion, vagrancy, and perjury. What the police were suspicious of was never made clear. On the face of it, Capone, with his ostentatious display of diamonds, was no vagrant. But Miami law tried to get around that by holding that people of means could be classified as vagrants if they threatened the public peace and safety or were known gangsters. The perjury count stemmed from Capone's charges of mistreatment while under arrest. He claimed that the authorities refused him food and water, threatened his family with arrest, denied him the opportunity to call his attorney, and vowed to throw his valuables down the toilet. Once again Capone's attorneys won the day for him. Capone had done nothing wrong in Miami to warrant jail or banishment. Essentially, the judge ruled that it was not a crime to be an undesirable. If people didn't want to associate with him, they need not do so. That many did was evidence of accepting him for his charm or money, perhaps both.[4]

In actuality, Capone never moved to take over in Miami. He wanted a vacation to get away from the stress and strain of the fast and dangerous life he had in Chicago. However, he could not do that completely. Unlike his life in Chicago, in which he had a business office and a family home far removed from the scene, his villa in Miami served both purposes. He was often calling Chicago, receiving mob members at his villa, and entertaining socially on Palm Island. His active social life certainly restricted any widespread business activity locally. What little he engaged in threatened no one. Since many who opposed him were into gambling and selling liquor, they were not much better morally. Thus, the opposition to him seems to have been motivated by the fear of competition, political intrigue whereby party hopefuls could make a name for themselves at his expense, and class/ethnic prejudice. Capone had survived the murderous Prohibition gang wars of Chicago. Toughened and single-minded, he was up to whatever the Miamians could throw at him.[5]

NOTES

1. Cited in Fred D. Pasley, *Al Capone: The Biography of a Self-Made Man* (1930; reprint, Freeport, N.Y., 1971), p. 159.

2. Ibid., p. 352.

3. Cited in John K. Kobler, *Capone: The Life and World of Al Capone* (New York, 1971), pp. 216–17.

4. Laurence Bergreen, *Capone: The Man and the Era* (New York, 1994), p. 662; Kobler, *Capone*, pp. 219–23, 290–93; Robert J. Schoenberg, *Mr. Capone* (New York, 2001), pp. 261–73.

5. Kobler, *Capone*, passim; Pasley, *Capone*, passim.

Al Capone. Library of Congress.

George "Bugs" Moran. Library of Congress.

Gabby Hartnett, a star player for the Chicago Cubs, autographs a baseball for Al Capone and his son at a charity baseball game in 1931. Library of Congress.

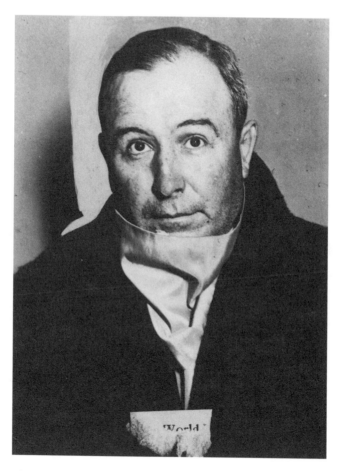

Johnny Torrio, 1931. Library of Congress.

Lucky Luciano, 1935. Library of Congress.

Frank Nitti, 1932. Library of Congress.

A 1931 cartoon. Library of Congress.

Al Capone, in 1932, on the train to the federal penitentiary in Atlanta, Georgia. John Binder, personal collection.

Capone, when he was arrested for the Christmas Day 1925
shootings in Brooklyn of the Irish White Hand gangsters. John
Binder, personal collection.

Capone in Miami, Florida, in 1941 with his lawyer Abe Teitelbaum. John Binder, personal collection.

Aftermath of St. Valentine's Day massacre, February 14, 1929. John Binder, personal collection.

Chapter 9

CAPONE AT LEISURE

Despite the many responsibilities that went with heading Chicago's most powerful gang, Capone found time for rest and rehabilitation when needed. Always surrounded by a bevy of bodyguards, he was able to take vacations, relax, and enjoy himself in many ways.

Not a good athlete, though he did excel at pool, he enjoyed playing golf. Able to hit a long drive, he was plagued by hooking the ball and erratic putting. At first, he seldom broke 60 for 9 holes; he eventually increased to playing 18 holes, though there is no evidence that he was ever anything but a hacker on the golf course. His rounds were devoted to having fun with his gangster friends, who drank plenty on each hole, gambled recklessly on the stroke of a ball, and carried loaded weapons in their golf bags for use in emergencies.

Essentially, though, Capone loved sports as a spectator. He attended sporting events as often as possible: baseball games, boxing matches, and horse and dog races. A Chicago Cubs baseball fan, he was a regular at their home games, usually accompanied by politicians who were not afraid to be seen as his guests in his box seat. He loved to watch boxing matches and spent many an hour at the local gyms where boxers worked out in anticipation of an upcoming match. Occasionally, he would step into a ring and spar with friends. He and Jack Dempsey, the heavyweight champion of the world, were close friends and had a healthy respect for each other. When Dempsey retired, he became a fight promoter for Capone. The job lasted until Dempsey had to tell a boxer to throw a fight. The Manassa Mauler, as Dempsey was known, eventually went to Miami Beach and worked with Meyer Lansky in running the Dempsey/Vander-

bilt Hotel there. Capone had weekly luncheons for the press to discuss upcoming matches and often gave parties after the fights, which were heavily attended by politicians and society luminaries. The attendees were
treated to alcoholic drinks, plenty of food, the latest jazz groups, and the
best cigars available. Since many high-society people attended the fights,
boxing proved to be one way for gangsters to mix with the elites and gain
some upward social mobility. An inveterate gambler, Capone always bet
on the local favorites. Barney Ross, who eventually became a champion
in three classes (lightweight, junior welterweight, and welterweight) was
probably the best known among them.

A number of sportswriters who attended Capone's weekly meetings included the acerbic Westbrook Pegler, who later gained a reputation as a
hard-hitting journalist; Paul Gallico, an Italian American author highly
regarded for his short stories; and Damon Runyon. Runyon was close to
Capone. Hanging out with the gangster element, Runyon undoubtedly got
much material for his short stories, which have become legend in American literature and served as themes in many motion pictures. Runyon observed gangsters up close and saw them as flawed individuals who cared
deeply for those "guys and dolls" in the straight world who needed help in
their quest to get by. He portrayed not so much their ruthless treatment of
their rivals as their compassionate concern for the underdogs.

Capone had proprietary and sporting interests in horse and dog tracks
and gambling emporiums. He had a piece of the action at the Hawthorne
Race Track in Cicero as well as the Ship. At both places, he was often
seen wagering hundreds and thousands of dollars. One biographer, Laurence Bergreen, states that the track offered fixed races and consequently
Capone always knew which horse would win. The implication is clear
that he always won on the races. In the same breath, the writer states that
Capone was also a loser, in that he would drop tens of thousands of dollars
on the roll of the dice, as testimony to the legitimacy of gambling establishments in Cicero.[1] While it is true that races have been fixed, it is also
certain that only a small percentage of them qualify as "boat races." The
purpose of fixing a race is to make a big score—that is, to win a lot of
money on the one race. That takes time to set up, as we shall soon see.

Horse racing is a universal, age-old sport, known for centuries as the
sport of kings. English colonists brought it to America, and America's
elite, including some presidents, owned and raced horses. Owners ran
their horse flesh, standardbreds (trotters and pacers) or thoroughbreds
guided by jockeys, either in country lanes and small tracks in rural venues
or in big city ovals. The horse business was a gamble at best. Like buying
a used car today, one never knows what he or she is really getting. Race

horses are no different. Owners and trainers often try to hide the horses' condition from the potential buyer or bettor. They want to hide a horse's form—that is, its performance ability—so as to receive the most return at the betting window or from a bookie. But there are other factors. Jockeys may work at cross-purposes with the owners and trainers in the hope of making a score. Grooms, who are the caretakers of the animals, may be persuaded to alter the horse's condition by changing their daily routines. Placing judges, those who determine the order of finish of a race, in the days before cameras were placed at the finish line for photo finishes, might declare the wrong horse a winner, deliberately or otherwise. Add to that mix the fact that horses are not machines. They can feel great one day and downright sluggish the next. No one can tell for sure until after the race is run. And horses are very strong. Even the strongest, most talented, and gifted jockeys can not always control a horse if the horse has a head to run or not run. Thus, trainers who order a jockey to ride not to win for a few races, in the hope that the horse will be a long shot in the future, have no assurance that the animal will perform optimally when asked to do so. The point is that there are so many ways to try to fix a race and so many things that can go wrong with one's plan to do so that there is no sure thing in racing. The best one can hope for is that all involved in racing a horse on a given day will do their best to win. It is highly unlikely, then, that Capone always knew who would win a race. Bergreen claims that Capone's reliance on inside information at Hawthorne dulled his handicapping skills. Presumably this cost him dearly when he went to Florida and attended Hialeah Race Track and lost heavily. But that hardly mattered to Capone. What was important was his being there. He readily greeted well-wishers at the track as he paraded around with a glamorous companion on each arm as bodyguards nearby kept an ever-watchful eye to insure their safety. It was a scene that Lucky Luciano would re-create years later when, deported to Italy, he would frequent Agnano Racetrack outside of Naples. The attractive women and the bodyguards were ever-present as were the well-wishers. For Capone and Luciano, his old buddy from New York, the races provided the setting and the occasion to massage the ego, to make sure that the people knew who was number one.

Bergreen also implies that Capone's losses at gambling were done to show potential customers that gambling was on the level in Cicero. At his income tax evasion trial, Capone claimed to have lost, from 1926 to 1929, hundreds of thousands of dollars gambling, most of it on horses. The simplest explanation is usually the right one. It is more likely that Capone lost hundreds of thousands of dollars not because of some complicated scheme to attract customers but because he had little regard for money, which he demonstrated on numerous occasions, was a really bad gambler, and was an atrociously inept horseplayer.

Capone also enjoyed playing poker with friends and acquaintances: bookies, prize-fighters, fight promoters, and their wives. There is no evidence that he was any better at that than shooting dice, at which he was known to lose as much as $10,000 on a roll, or any other form of gambling.

A man of many interests, Capone loved opera and had an extensive record collection that provided him enormous pleasure. He especially appreciated Giuseppe Verdi's works and the performances of the great Italian tenor Enrico Caruso. He would take their records to his country hideaway in Long Lake, near Lansing, Michigan, and listen joyously as he identified with the fictional heroes of song, seeing himself as a paladin defending the freedom, equal opportunities, and honor of his fellow Italian Americans. The Big Fellow also enjoyed swimming, lolling about, and socializing with the natives, especially the youngsters, who brought out the best in him. Long Lake also had a roadhouse nearby where single girls on the make made themselves available for 10 cents a dance and some drinks. Capone latched on to a stunning blonde beauty whom he chose as his mistress. She would be available when he would return for vacations from time to time. Keeping women on the side was second nature to him whether at his headquarters in the Metropole Hotel, the Lexington Hotel, or wherever he might be staying for any length of time.

There wasn't much that Capone didn't do for amusement. He attended the theater and was particularly fond of Harry Richman, the showman. He threw lavish parties. He thoroughly enjoyed jazz, the new music coming from New Orleans and Kansas City, which attracted those who would become giants in the field. Among them were Louis Armstrong, trumpeter extraordinaire; Milt Hinton, the premier bassist; and Jelly Roll Morton, songwriter, self-proclaimed inventor of jazz, and probably the best jazz pianist in the country. There was also Duke Ellington and King Oliver, band leader trumpeter from New Orleans who brought Armstrong to Chicago. Many of them worked in his saloons, which were the principal source of employment for them in the 1920s. Many of the artists knew of Capone's reputation and were uneasy, if not downright scared, to play in his clubs. But most of them came to appreciate the gigs and see him as a gregarious, friendly, generous impresario. Pianist-songwriter Fats Waller was "kidnapped" one time and brought to play at Capone's birthday party, which lasted for three days. He soon got over his fear when Capone started stashing hundred-dollar bills into the pianist's pockets. All in all Waller made thousands of dollars and came away feeling a symbiotic relationship with Capone, who loved to live it up as much as Waller loved to play.

If you worked in clubs owned by the Capone gang or one of its members, you were expected to be loyal to your employer. The comic Joe E. Lewis found this out the hard way. He left Machine Gun Jack McGurn's club for one run by the Moran gang and was lucky to survive to tell about it. McGurn knifed him, nearly killing the comic. Clarinetist Milton "Mezz" Mezzrow was a favorite of Capone, who expected him to help make bootleg liquor when needed. On one occasion, Capone noticed that his younger brother Matthew was very interested in Mezzrow's female singer. Capone told Mezz to fire her. Claiming she was a good singer, Mezz refused. Capone let it slide with the admonition that if Matthew were seen around the club it wouldn't be good for him or the clarinet player. Mezzrow got the message.[2]

Capone's relationships with entertainers went beyond being in their company and enjoying their performances. A Jekyll and Hyde, he probably learned about drugs from the jazz world and sampled some, yet he often preached family values to the players. He especially advised the younger ones to get their religious education, keep in touch regularly with their parents, send their mothers flowers, and give the moms and dads the love and respect due them.[3] Perhaps it was his concern for the entertainers and their families that made them feel wanted and needed. They chose to value the good side of Capone and block out the bad. The case of Milt Hinton is testimony to that. Splintered with glass in an automobile accident while delivering booze to one of Capone's customers, he was rushed to the hospital with his key digit for bass playing hanging in the balance. The doctor wanted to amputate, but Capone, being there with Hinton, said no. Following Capone's advice, the doctor sewed the finger back on well enough that Hinton, in a career that spanned close to 70 years, became the most recorded musician of all time playing bass for innumerable bands and small groups. Hinton died in 2000 at age 90, ever-grateful to Capone for giving him an opportunity to play, for picking up the medical bills, and for being instrumental in saving his finger. Capone showed a compassion not generally associated with violent gangsters.[4]

Capone's association with jazz musicians brought him into close contact with African Americans, whom he judged by the value of their talent, not the color of their skin. He took the same attitude in building his empire. Some of the jazz musicians, black and white, fleetingly dabbled in bootlegging. Capone was willing to take them in regardless of race. He organized African American bootleggers, gave them police protection, and increased their profits. In return, they were expected to buy their alcohol from him and only him. He enjoyed a rapport with them that was years ahead of his time.[5]

Capone took to boating and boasted of owning a yacht and a sleek 40-foot cabin cruiser that had been built by Ransom E. Olds, the founder of Oldsmobile. The boat could do 40 knots, slept four, and had the usual conveniences of home, including a kitchen and shower. He used it to go fishing or for joyrides, which his son Sonny enjoyed immensely. He also entertained guests on the boat, and often took short trips to the Bahamas, where he and his entourage might go to dine and socialize with friends.[6]

As a young man Capone drank heavily, but brought his habit under control after his mother and wife joined him in Chicago in 1923. His social life, as mentioned previously, was a contributing factor to his addiction to cocaine. He became a user, as did many in the high society to which he aspired.

In sum, Capone lived his leisure life to the fullest. He made it a point to ingratiate himself to as many people as possible, treating them with respect and generosity. It paid off for him. Wherever Capone went he was usually treated like a celebrity, glad-handed by scores of people who were eager to shake his hand and wish him well. He had a coterie of loyal friends who stuck by him. Bergreen wrote of Capone that he had an ability to get people to "overlook his scandalous reputation," and to pretend that Capone "had nothing to do with violence or sexual degradation." Moreover, Capone could "evoke this suspension of disbelief...a skill normally belonging to an expert politician." The result was "akin to a mass hallucination...for he [Capone] managed to replace...the terrible things they said about him...with a new version of the truth."[7] This was true up until the time he was to stand trial for income tax evasion. Then, those among the general public who were willing to look the other way at his criminal doings began to turn against him.

NOTES

1. Laurence Bergreen, *Capone: The Man and the Era* (New York, 1994), p. 100.

2. Ibid., pp. 249–51.

3. Ibid., pp. 259–60.

4. Milt Hinton, interviewed under the direction of Monk Rowe, video recording, Hamilton College Jazz Archive, Hamilton, N.Y., May 31, 1995. Hinton's interview is one of more than 200 videotaped and on file at that archive. Rowe told this author on September 13, 2000, that he remembers the details of the Capone/Hinton relationship as portrayed in this text al-

though all of them many not be on the video tape. See also Bergreen, *Capone: The Man*, pp. 245–48.

5. Bergreen, *Capone: The Man*, p. 248.

6. Owners of the cabin cruiser, conversation with author, 2 August 2002. The cruiser is currently in dry dock undergoing renovations in the Thousand Islands and should be ready to relaunch in the summer of 2004. The owners prefer to remain anonymous.

7. Bergreen, *Capone: The Man*, p. 260.

Chapter 10

THE TRIAL: PART 1

Talk to most any inmate of a maximum-security prison and they will tell you that they are innocent of the crime for which they are doing time. It is not that they are claiming to be innocent babes in the woods, simply that since the government can't convict them for something that they did, prosecutors settle on trumped-up charges. A somewhat similar scenario holds true for Al Capone. This is not to claim that he didn't evade taxes. Rather, the government considered him a menace to society and did all it could to put him away, even to the point of intimidating witnesses.

Capone had a worldwide reputation as a feared killer, yet the law was unable to convict him of any murders. Eyewitnesses developed amnesia or disappeared completely. No one was willing to testify against him in open court. The government, especially the U.S. government, was extremely frustrated that Capone was on the loose for so long. It was certain that Capone was violating the Volstead Act prohibiting the sale of alcohol, but could not prove it. Not even Elliot Ness and his Untouchables could stop Capone from running and peddling booze and beer, to say nothing of their inability to gather sufficient evidence to send him to federal prison. The government concluded that it had the best chance of putting Capone away by convicting him of income tax evasion.

Tax evasion was predicated on the avoidance of payment due on earned income. In other words, the government had to prove that one had taxable income in order to prosecute successfully. In the 1920s the threshold was $5,000. Today, workers pay withholding taxes before they even get their regular salaries. The government knows how much each employee earns and pays in taxes. Self-employed persons must file regular reports detailing their income. But during Prohibition there was no withholding system. Capone could and did say that he drew a salary working for Torrio and thus show some income that was not necessarily taxable. The government had to prove otherwise.

Prior to 1927, people who made money illegally saw no need to declare it. They cited their Fifth Amendment right against self-incrimination. In 1927, however, the U.S. Supreme Court ruled in the Sullivan decision that illegal income was reportable and taxable. The argument of jeopardizing one's constitutional right against self-incrimination was rejected. This ruling hit hard against bootlegging and gambling, two industries in which Capone and hundreds of gangsters were heavily invested. Before long, the federal government unleashed a flurry of tax-related charges against many infamous characters in the rackets. One by one, they were convicted of income tax evasion and served time. Ralph Capone, Terry Druggan, Frankie Lake, Jack Guzik, and Frank Nitti were among those indicted, convicted, fined, and imprisoned. Their sentences ranged from 18 months to 3 years. It took the government four years from start to finish before they put Druggan and Lake away. Ralph Capone had the opportunity to settle for $4,000 in taxes owed for income of roughly $70,000 from 1922 to 1925. After signing the agreement, he refused to pay, claiming he lacked the necessary funds due to losses in investments and gambling. His poor judgment and miserliness cost him his freedom. He served just over two years in a federal prison.

The government had made easy cases against the gangsters who left a trail of income. Al Capone was much craftier. He showed no income to speak of. He owned no property; never endorsed a check; signed no receipts; had no bank account. He paid cash for everything. He was a master at concealing his financial transactions. Barring making a prima facie case of Capone's annual revenue—that is, having an adequate factual basis for prosecution—the feds would have to demonstrate that his lifestyle required a certain income beyond what he claimed. Then they had to convince a jury of his peers that Capone had earned this taxable revenue.

There was an ironic twist to the events leading up to Capone's trial. Aiding the overall drive against Capone was the Secret Six, a group of wealthy Chicagoans who contributed close to a million dollars to the Chicago Crime Commission and the IRS in the hope that they would bring down Capone. One of the secret group was Samuel Insull, who would later be exposed and convicted as a utilities and corporate marauder with few peers in American history. The sociologist E. Digby

Baltzell viewed Capone as relatively innocent alongside Insull, who seduced and bought political and civic figures. Citing Kenneth Allsop, a chronicler of the prohibition era, Baltzell claimed that Insull represented "the great abandonment of honesty and integrity in public life... that had as a by-product the moral climate in which Capone ascended."[1]

These hometown efforts were slow to bear fruit. Concerned citizens were demoralized by the inability of local and state authorities to deal effectively with Capone and turned to the newly elected President Herbert Hoover. Though the federal government, generally, had no authority over Capone's possible involvement in murder, gambling, and prostitution, it knew he was vulnerable in bootlegging and income tax issues. Capone had admitted to being a bootlegger and had never filed a federal tax return. Hoover ordered federal agents to do what had to be done to put Capone behind bars.

Working out of the Justice Department, Elliot Ness put together a group of individuals he had picked for their special skills and honesty. He was not disappointed. His men disrupted Capone's operation and managed to put a mole into Capone's gang. Ness thrived on the popularity he gained from his efforts. Yet they brought no conviction. Neither did they dry up Chicago nor stop Capone from operating. Later, Ness wrote a book about his squad's exploits, aptly named *The Untouchables*. Made into a television series, it featured excessive violence and bloodshed. Viewers were thrilled by his men raiding warehouses with machine guns blazing and busting up barrels of beer and booze, which flowed like rivulets into Chicago's streets and sewers. Many viewers believed it to be an accurate portrayal of Ness's work against Capone, the Mafia, and organized crime. In reality, it was pure fantasy and ironic. For all his honesty, Ness, who reveled in being a crusader against the Wets, had a serious drinking problem. It would, later on, ruin his career and multiple marriages. As for the gunplay, those close to Ness claimed he never carried a weapon in Chicago and, if he did, he never drew it out of its holster. In fairness to Ness, he did not originally write a gory shoot-'em-up story, but was convinced to change his tale if he wanted his book to sell. A scholar's comments on the achievements of a colleague capture the Ness story well: "it doesn't matter what you do, what... matters is what you pretend to do."[2] Ness was a great pretender. The public bought his story hook, line, and sinker.

From 1927 on, the feds began a process that would eventually put Capone out of business for failure to pay his income tax. Spurred on by the Sullivan decision, Elmer L. Irey, Chief Enforcement Officer of the IRS, successfully targeted a number of Chicago's bootleggers well before President Hoover's drive to get Capone. When Hoover directed Irey to move against Capone in January 1929, Irey confidently put together a team, which included Frank Wilson and Michael F. Malone. Wilson had proven himself in getting convictions against Druggan and Lake. Malone had no peer as an undercover agent. Irey's team worked day and night. They sought to establish a case based on "net worth" and "net expenditure." If they could prove that Capone was spending more than he was taking in, the money he spent beyond his means could be declared unreported and therefore taxable. After pouring over his outlays for foods and services from 1926 to 1929 and adding in his fixed possessions, they came up with about $165,000 of taxable income. Given the assumption that Capone was taking in up to $100 million some years, the amount seemed trivial. Yet it made the case against Capone possible.

The legality of such a net worth case was still to be decided by the Supreme Court. Would all this work in tracing Capone's tracks in hotels, restaurants, retail stores of every imaginable kind, real estate offices, automobile dealerships, boat dealers, and others be in vain? Wilson and company wanted some hard-and-fast data on Capone's ownership of the sources of his immense income: the breweries, the distilleries, the gambling casinos, and the houses of prostitution. Despite some promising leads fed to Wilson by a hooker he had persuaded to work for him, and from his spy Michael Malone, the government still lacked the solid evidence it felt it needed to bring an airtight case against Capone. A major stumbling block was that those who could supply that kind of damaging information against Capone would not do so for fear of retaliation. Others were simply not sympathetic to the government's move against the bootleggers or were part of Capone's organization and had no desire to, essentially, testify against themselves.

In April 1930, Lawrence P. Mattingly, Capone's attorney, informed Wilson that Capone desired to clear up his tax problems. They were willing to settle. They met. They talked. Wilson opened with what is termed today a "Miranda warning" against self-incrimination. Mattingly countered with a standard statement used in settlement cases to the effect that whatever was said would be without admitting Capone's liability to criminal action. Capone offered that he kept no records and was in the employ of Johnny Torrio prior to 1926. He declined to answer all of the pointed questions directed at getting to the bottom of his income. But the wheels of justice were set in motion.

Assuming his statement protected his client against any incriminating information and expecting the government to accept some kind of plea which would carry a lenient judgment against Capone, Mattingly presented a statement detailing his estimates of Capone's income to Wilson. It stipulated that from 1926 through 1929 Capone made not more than $266,000.

As it turned out, Mattingly had seriously miscalculated. He believed the actions to be a civil case, one that would be settled in an agreement between the two parties. That being so, his actions made sense. Precedent was on his side. The government had always settled rather than prosecuted in such cases. What he failed to realize was the government's determination to bring a criminal suit against Capone. The admission of Capone's income, if allowed to be introduced in a criminal case, would establish the base for a net worth case against him.[3]

Matters came to a head in June 1931, when a federal grand jury indicted Capone on 22 felony counts of income tax evasion and 2 misdemeanor charges for failure to file. A week later it charged Capone with violating the Prohibition laws. But the tax case took precedence. Since the government's case was largely circumstantial unless it could prove Capone had earned income, the Mattingly statement was crucial to a successful prosecution. Mattingly gave the government the starting point needed to demonstrate that Capone lived beyond his means. Since the prosecution was not certain the Mattingly statement would be admitted as evidence, it agreed to a plea bargain with the defense. In essence, the prosecution and defense negotiated a deal whereby Capone would plead guilty to charges in exchange for a sentence acceptable to both parties. Judge James Wilkerson set sentencing for June 30. Plea-bargaining was a standard procedure in tax cases as well as other types of cases. By reducing the number of trials by juries, it guarantees some punishment for the criminal and helps to maintain a viable court system, which might otherwise break down from the weight of too many trials. Its detractors claim it is flawed by letting off criminals with lighter sentences than they deserve or encouraging innocent people to plead guilty to avoid lengthy and/or intimidating trials. It remains an integral part of America's justice system.

Theoretically, Capone could receive over 30 years in prison and almost $100,000 in fines. Practically, however, the most ever given for a guilty plea for tax evasion had been 18 months. Mike Ahearn, who was now serving as Capone's attorney, got a continuance until July 30 so that Capone could attend to some legal matters in Florida.

July 30, 1931, spelled the beginning of the end for Al Capone. Though President Hoover was pleased that Capone was finally being brought to some kind of justice, Capone saw the plea bargain as a victory of sorts. He was cheerfully telling people that he would get no more than two or three years. The press questioned the character of the justice system, and the public across the nation perceived that Capone had reached Judge Wilkerson. The jurist would have none of that. From the opening statement on, Judge Wilkerson made it clear that he was not bound by any plea bargain between the prosecution and the defense.

The deal was off. Judge Wilkerson allowed Capone to withdraw his guilty pleas on taxes, but pressed the grand jury to change the Prohibition indictment beyond conspiracy, thereby exposing Capone to a much longer sentence if found guilty as charged. The jury did not have the evidence to do that. Capone withdrew his guilty plea and never did stand trial on the Prohibition charges. He would, however, have to defend himself on the tax charges. Trial was set for October 6, 1931.[4]

NOTES

1. E. Digby Baltzell, *The Protestant Establishment: Aristocracy and Caste in America* (New York, 1964), p. 218.

2. Professor Joseph Velikonja, letter to the author, 6 June 2001.

3. Robert J. Schoenberg, *Mr. Capone* (New York, 2001), pp. 256–60. Schoenberg takes an insightful look at the Capone trial and the American Bar Association's mock trial held 30 years later.

4. Ibid., pp. 303–15.

Chapter 11
THE TRIAL: PART 2

Capone was accustomed to being cheered when he attended public events. Now that the government was bringing income tax evasion charges against him crowds started booing him. Was it a bad omen? If so, he sought foolproof ways to avoid incarceration or, if need be, fix the outcome of the trial. He had often bribed people to get what he wanted. This time no one was willing to guarantee that he wouldn't do time. Still, if he could buy off the jury he wouldn't have to be concerned with a stretch in federal prison. Capone set out to reach enough jurors to insure that he would be found innocent. Enter Ed O'Hare.[1]

Edward J. O'Hare was a young attorney from St. Louis who had managed to gain control of patent rights to the mechanical rabbits that dog tracks used to get greyhound dogs to chase around the track. Because dog racing was illegal throughout the country, track owners were mostly gangsters. Capone himself had a share in the Hawthorne Kennel Club near Cicero. O'Hare was getting rich off his business with the mobsters, but considered himself too good to associate with them despite his own criminal actions. O'Hare had been convicted of stealing hundreds of dollars worth of liquor from a fellow tenant named George Remus. O'Hare appealed the conviction, which was overturned when Remus withdrew his damaging testimony. Later it was revealed O'Hare had bought off Remus.[2]

Realizing the huge profit potential in dog tracks, O'Hare started the Madison Kennel Club across the river from St. Louis. He made a small fortune until the police shut him down. Since he had the rights to the mechanical rabbit, he used that as a lever to enter into partnership with Capone in the Hawthorne Kennel Club. The mobsters were quick to rec-

ognize O'Hare's abilities as an attorney and executive and gave him the
go-ahead to operate dog tracks in Florida and Massachusetts.[3] Little did
they know the trouble he would cause them, especially Capone.

O'Hare became a successful entrepreneur. He became owner or a high
executive in a number of diverse businesses having to do with horse racing
(Sportsman's Park), pro football (the Chicago Cardinals), real estate and
insurance companies, and advertising agencies. He was an excellent example of the sociologist Daniel Bell's classic theory that "crime is a queer ladder of social mobility."[4] But he wanted more. He wanted his son, Edward
Henry O'Hare, to go to Annapolis. Figuring that informing on Capone
would be a surefire way to help Edward get an appointment, he became a
mole for Frank Wilson. Wilson called O'Hare his most valuable informer.
Meanwhile, Edward Henry O'Hare went to Annapolis, graduated, became
an ace pilot in World War II, and died a hero, shot down in aerial combat.
He is memorialized in Chicago with the airport that bears his name.[5]

It was O'Hare who tipped off the prosecution that Capone had
arranged to bribe a number of jurors slated to be on Judge Wilkerson's
panel. Advised of the potential problem, Wilkerson told the prosecution
to go ahead with their case and leave the jury matter to him. His solution
was as brilliant as it was sly. On the day the trial was to begin, he switched
panels with another judge. From that time on the jurors were sequestered
and out of reach of Capone and his men. They would be free to vote as
they saw the evidence. They could not be coerced.

The jury was essentially rural in nature. Representing the "Drys"—that
is, those in favor of virtuous America and enforcing Prohibition laws—it
would not take kindly to "Wets," those who were not mindful of Prohibition and were seeking its repeal. In the eyes of the Drys, the Wets symbol-
ized the darker side of urban America. Making matters worse, the Wet on
trial was a descendant of Italian immigrants, who since the 1880s, in
Chicago especially, had been marked as a people with foreboding criminal
tendencies. From a rural WASP juror's point of view, Capone had three
strikes against him from the start. He was big city, Italian, and Catholic.
The panel was hardly a jury of Capone's peers. As one observant individual
remarked, a panel that would include those suspected of murder and mayhem would not be fit legally to stand as jurors. But, in the broader sense, em-
powering city people who would have been more representative of the Wet
attitudes would have given Capone a better chance to defend himself.[6]

O'Hare liked undercover work so much that he informed on others be-
sides Capone. Eventually his double life caught up with him. He never got
to know the glory of his son. In November 1939, two men drove alongside
O'Hare's automobile and filled it full of shotgun fire.[7]

The government's case opened with an IRS witness who claimed that Al Capone did not file income tax returns from 1924 to 1929. The prosecution then presented testimony to prove that Capone owned the gambling casino known as the Hawthorne Smoke Shop. The evidence left no doubt that the operation was overwhelmingly successful. Bookkeeper Leslie Shumway stated that for two years profits totaled close to $550,000. He could not say for certain that Capone was the head man. He did believe that Capone walked around as though he was the boss. In effect, a circumstantial case was made against Capone, rather than one beyond a shadow of a doubt.

Then the prosecution introduced the Mattingly letter, the key to convicting Capone. The defense objected. It argued that the government had encouraged tax delinquents to bargain with it to avoid criminal or civil action. Capone attorney Albert Fink claimed that statements made to plea-bargain could not be used against the defendant in trial.[8] Fink was on the right track, but did not press the argument sufficiently. The law held that bona fide offers to plea bargain could not be used as evidence.[9] Rather, Fink followed up with an attempt to show that Mattingly was ignorant of the law and incompetent, which, if true, would nullify the bona fide offer to compromise, thereby making the Mattingly statement admissible. No matter, Judge Wilkerson allowed it. The letter set a base figure for Capone's income. If the government could show that Capone's spending exceeded his admitted income, it had a powerful case of income tax evasion. The stage was set. The prosecution would show how much money Capone really made.

The government had worked for years amassing evidence against Capone and easily documented its case. Its agents had traced Capone's tracks and interviewed scores of merchants and businessmen with whom he had dealt. Witness after witness testified to Capone's lavish lifestyle. They portrayed him as having a passion for squandering money. Capone kept rooms at two Chicago hotels, the Metropole and the Lexington. He often booked extra rooms to entertain visiting friends whom he invited to attend sporting events. He shopped often in Florida at the butcher shop, the bakery, the furniture and carpet stores, the tailor shops, and the haberdashers. He spent more on meat and pastries in a week than ordinary people could spend in a year. Ever ready to renovate and keep up his Palm Isle estate, he poured thousands of dollars into maintaining it. His telephone bill was incomprehensible to the average citizen. He spent over $3,000 in calls in 1929 alone. He annually donated as much as $70,000 to churches and the police widows' and orphans' fund.[10]

The government had no trouble convincing rational people that Capone threw enormous sums of money around carelessly. It was what Capone made that was difficult to prove. As mentioned above, Shumway had testified to profits in the Hawthorne Smoke Shop, but presented no clear evidence that Capone owned it. Fred Ries turned out to be a star witness. A cashier in Capone's gambling operations, he implied strongly that Capone had interests in profitable gambling operations. Both men had testified under coercion. IRS agent Frank J. Wilson threatened to give up Shumway to Capone's men, who would surely kill him if they knew he would testify against their leader. Wilson used similar fear tactics against Ries. Knowing Ries had a mortal fear of insects, Wilson placed him in a very bug-infested cell until the terrified cashier agreed to cooperate.[11] Parker Henderson swore that he picked up money at Western Union so Capone could buy and remodel his Palm Island home.[12] John Fotre, the manager of Western Union at the Lexington Hotel, wired money to Capone, but could not remember who the sender was. He later claimed that he was being intimidated by Phil D'Andrea, the president of the *Unione Siciliana*, who eventually did six months in jail for carrying a gun in court.[13]

Defense attorney Ahern had objected to the monotonous recital of Capone's expenses on the grounds that they did not prove income. Judge Wilkerson overruled him with the admonition that what he spent he must have taken in. In effect, rather than calling for proof of earned taxable income, the judge assumed it.

The defense was weak. Counting on a plea bargain, Fink and Ahern never considered a defense strategy. They asked for a few days to prepare a defense and got only a few hours. They based their case on the fact that Capone lost virtually all of his gambling house income to bookmakers. They presented a case that lacked specifics. They could not account for any additional income to pay for his possessions and expenditures beyond $200,000. Nor did the defense make much sense legally. Gambling losses can only be deducted from gambling winnings. Fink and Ahern stressed that Capone was a habitual loser. In reality, the gambling defense was irrelevant.

In summation, Fink stressed that Capone believed that gambling income was nontaxable. When he realized it was, he tried to pay his taxes. He never had the intent to defraud the government. Ahern added that the government's evidence only shows that Capone was a spendthrift. He asked the jury to consider that Capone was being prosecuted and persecuted by those, especially the press, who considered him to be morally unfit.[14]

The prosecution summed up by saying that Capone was no Robin Hood. He spent wildly on himself and his cronies, not on the weak, the hungry, and the homeless who eked out a living by sleeping outdoors under overpasses and begged money from passersby, especially tourists who made their way to Florida seeking rest and relaxation in the salubrious ambience of the Miami area.

Judge Wilkerson, then, charged the jury. He explained the net worth argument. He advised that the Mattingly letter may be used if the jury concluded that Mattingly was authorized legally to get the information and use it in defense of Capone against the IRS.

The jury deliberated for eight hours. Its verdict puzzled many. It voted not guilty on the first indictment and most of the other counts of tax evasion. But, most damaging to Capone, it found him guilty on three counts of evasion for 1925–27 and two counts of failure to file a return for 1928 and 1929. His attorneys appealed on the grounds that the indictments did not specify the means used by Capone to evade taxes.[15]

On October 24, 1931, Judge Wilkerson sentenced Capone to 11 years imprisonment and fined him $50,000 plus court costs of $30,000. It was the harshest sentence ever given out for tax evasion. Fink and Ahern, who had appealed the decision, requested that Capone be freed on bail pending the appeal. Wilkerson denied bail to Capone. The IRS immediately placed a lien on his property and froze his assets to insure payment of taxes owed.

Housed in Cook County Jail, Capone was able to use his contacts to make his stay comfortable, if not pleasurable. Warden David Moneypenny was sympathetic to Capone. He assigned him to a private cell with a shower and gave him access to a telephone and Western Union. Political friends obtained passes to visit him and gave them to the likes of Johnny Torrio, Jack Guzik, Murray Humphreys, and other gang members. Torrio raised cash to help Capone pay for the many expenses incurred in the trial and arranged to have Lucky Luciano and Dutch Schultz visit Capone. Exhibiting a warped sense of humor, Capone got a vicarious thrill as he sat in the jail's electric chair and discussed mob business with the visiting New Yorkers. Hoping to lead a national organization some day, he tried to convince them to go along with him. Luciano said nothing. Schultz was not impressed. He adamantly spoke of going it alone, rather than being an important member of the team. Capone expected that Torrio would certainly side with him. It was not to be.[16]

Capone just did not get it. How could he get away with murderous deeds and be put away for something as frivolous (in his mind) as income tax evasion? His advancing syphilis had something to do with that. Moreover, it prevented him from knowing the reality of his loosening grip on gangland. His world was beginning to crumble around him and he still fantasized about grandiose, even Napoleonic, accomplishments of gangland leadership. The reality was that he had been artfully shunted aside at the Atlantic City meeting in 1929. Now, two years later, his life out in the open for all to see and a felony conviction hanging over his head, he was anathema to his gangland buddies. They did not want to humiliate him. Instead, they ignored him. They wanted no part of him.

Capone's charmed life in the Cook County Jail came to light eventually. U.S. government officials ordered an end to it. In December 1931, Moneypenny placed Capone in a hospital ward under 24-hour guard and limited his visitors to his mother, wife, son, and lawyers.[17]

On February 17, 1932, Capone learned that his appeal had been rejected. He then appealed to the U.S. Supreme Court, which turned him down in early May 1932. His family gave him a big send-off party. Mama Teresa brought a big bowl of pasta and all the trimmings from home, and with Mae, Sonny, Mafalda, and a number of Al's brothers, they shared it as the once invincible mobster prepared to embark on his trip to Atlanta Penitentiary.

Capone had tried innumerable ways to avoid federal prison. His last-gasp effort was offering to do his best to bring the kidnapped Lindbergh baby safely home. Government officials rejected it, as did Colonel Charles Lindbergh himself. Capone would soon find out, to his dismay, that Atlanta Penitentiary was not Cook County Jail.

Much has been made of Capone's trial. Like Monday morning quarterbacks, critics found fault with many of the decisions that the defense team made. They claimed that his attorneys were incompetent. They should have done this or that. In 1990 the American Bar Association (ABA), staged a mock trial. Using trial standards not applicable in the early 1930s, it brought out what were considered to be serious blunders. Mattingly should never had allowed Capone to attend the plea bargain conference. He should never have given statements after being told that whatever he said could be used against Capone. At the trial, the wrong attorney, Albert Fink, did the bulk of the courtroom work. Ahern's partner, Tommy Nash, was among the best courtroom lawyers. He didn't participate in the active proceedings. To this day, no one has ever explained why Nash didn't take the lead in the courtroom defense.[18] Though able, Fink did not come up to Nash's standards. The defense glossed over its best point, which was that the government was encouraging people to come forward and settle. Therefore, it acted arbitrarily and capriciously against Capone.

For what it was worth, jurors in the ABA's mock trial voted Capone not guilty. They believed the government did not document Capone's earned income. They held that Capone did not willfully evade taxes since he did not know he had to file, and concluded that the testimony of Shumway and Ries was coerced. In essence, the jurors viewed the government unfairly persecuting Capone. Some jurists commented that if the charges were brought against Capone in today's day and age, the case would never make it to the jury.[19]

What the critics missed was the futility of criticizing the case on its legal merits or on the quality of the defense effort. It is likely that not even an attorney with the track record of a Johnny Cochrane could have gotten an acquittal for Al Capone. The case should be approached not as an entity isolated from other events of the times, but as an integral part of what was going on in America at the time. Capone's criminality and notoriety helped convict him, as did his ethnicity and the tenor of the times. Fink was right when he placed Capone in a Carthaginian context. They both had to be destroyed.

The merits of the government's case were nigh on irrelevant. The judge and the jury were not disposed to giving Capone a fair trial. It is not so much that they were blatantly biased against him. It was more that they were imbued with a subtle societal prejudice that people were often unaware of. Everyone "knew" that Capone was "an evil man." How could he possibly not have intended to cheat the government out of its rightful share of his earned income? The background of the case and the milieu of antipathy to immigrants helped turn it into one of assumptions rather than a reading of hard, incontrovertible courtroom proof.

Americans had come to view Italian immigrants as undesirables. Official government studies and scholarly reports had identified them as prone to criminality, especially violent crime, and as strikebreakers opposing the labor movement in America. Reflecting the racial bias of the era, investigators criticized their housing as small, dirty, and in need of repair, and their grounds as unimpressive. They lamented that the women were abominable housekeepers. They painted a picture so dismal that the integrity of Italian Americans was open to question. Accused of not working to their potential, Italian Americans were seen as takers and not givers to society. To make matters worse, Americans pointed to the immigrants' slowness to adapt to their new surroundings and become citizens, their disinterest in education, and their flirtations with radicalism. These judgments were based on assumptions and did not square with reality. Although essentially off the mark, the perceptions had been nurtured and were buried deep in the hearts and minds of many a well-meaning citizen.

It was the lynching of 11 Italians in New Orleans in 1890 and the specter of the Mafia and Black Hand that burned an indelible mark of criminality on Italian Americans. Suspected of killing David C. Hennessey, the chief of police in that city, 14 Italians were indicted, 9 were tried, 6 were acquitted, and a mistrial was declared on the remaining 3. Certain of the Italians' guilt and spurred by talk of witness intimidation and jury fixing, a citizens' group executed 11 Italians. A grand jury justified the action. The press around the nation generally applauded the outrage. In a typical response, the *New York Times* held that the vigilantes took the only course available to stop the Mafia and its bloody practices.[20] The possibility that Hennessey was a victim of an internal department feud or of warring factions for the control of New Orleans's docks, facts that were well known at the time, was essentially ignored. Citizens around the country were put on alert to the Mafia's secret intentions to take over America. This was another example of Americans putting the blame for their problems on foreigners. Periodically, citizens would be reminded of the threat of this foreign evil designed to corrupt and destroy America. Italians would suffer indignities over the years because of this fear-mongering. Americans would be quick to believe the worst about them.

After World War I, radicalism burned brightly in the United States. A number of Italian immigrants became disciples of it. Among them were Nicola Sacco, a factory worker, and Bartolomeo Vanzetti, a fish peddler. On May 5, 1920, they were arrested and charged with the murder of two men in a payroll robbery in South Braintree, Massachusetts. Convicted in 1921, they were executed in 1927. Though their guilt or innocence is still debated, there is no doubt that prejudice played a major role in meting out "justice" to them. The bias against Italian Americans was compounded by the fear of radicalism, against which the United States had launched a major campaign. While many scholars believe that Sacco was probably guilty as charged, virtually all agree that Vanzetti was innocent. What makes the case important for understanding the dynamics of the Capone trial is that the entire cause célèbre took place during the rise to power of the Chicago gangster. The execution of Sacco and Vanzetti was still fresh in the minds of most Americans when the trial of their countryman Capone got underway.

Equally important, the lynching of Italians did not start or stop with the New Orleans incident. Mob violence first erupted against Italians in Buena Vista, Pennsylvania, as early as 1874. It continued in every decade through to 1914 and 1915, when lynchings and murders claimed the lives of two Italians in Willisville and Johnson City, both in Illinois. Chicagoans were hardly unaware of the general undesirable reputation of Italians, who were considered "lynchable." The violence directed against Italians and Italian Americans revealed that denial of justice was likely in the failure of local or state authorities to afford adequate protection to them. Moreover, perpetrators were not punished criminally or otherwise for violating the Italians, nor were the state or local authorities willing to secure indemnity for the wronged persons. What redress of grievances was accorded to them came later, through the diplomatic efforts of the representatives of the United States and Italy. It is clear that the Italian immigrants were second-class citizens, not due the civil rights that Americans enjoyed. Having absorbed these lessons, Americans could hardly be expected to be sensitive to the rights of foreigners as seen in the broad sense. Children of immigrants, and sometimes even grandchildren, often were taken for foreigners by virtue of their looks or their ethnic names. They usually could not expect to be treated as first-class citizens. Given this scenario, what chance did Al Capone have against any jury in America? Would a team of expert defense attorneys have been able to succeed where Fink and Ahern failed? It is doubtful. Capone was a highly visible criminal who belonged to a group of people considered to be inferior. The judge "knew" it. So did the prosecutors and the jury. Some commentators have opined that the defense was so inept because they were stalling for time, hoping against hope that something would turn up to make their case for their client. A more plausible explanation would be that the defense knew the futility of trying to get Capone off scot-free. They went through the motions as best they could.[21]

NOTES

1. Robert J. Schoenberg, *Mr. Capone* (New York, 2001), p. 316.
2. John K. Kobler, *Capone: The Life and World of Al Capone* (New York, 1971), p. 244.
3. Ibid., p. 245.
4. Daniel Bell, "Crime as an American Way of Life," *Antioch Review*, Vol. 13, (summer 1953): p. xiii.
5. Kobler, *Capone*, p. 340.
6. Schoenberg, *Mr. Capone*, pp. 287–325; Laurence Bergreen, *Capone: The Man and the Era* (New York, 1994), pp. 431–92; and Kobler, *Capone*, pp. 336–54 all deal effectively with Capone's trial.
7. Kobler, *Capone*, p. 340.
8. Ibid., p. 342.
9. Schoenberg, *Mr. Capone*, pp. 318–19.
10. Ibid., pp. 319–20.

11. Bergreen, *Capone: The Man*, p. 396.

12. Schoenberg, *Mr. Capone*, pp. 319–20.

13. Ibid., p. 327.

14. Kobler, *Capone*, p. 347.

15. Ibid., p. 349.

16. Ibid., pp. 352–53.

17. Ibid., p. 352.

18. Schoenberg, *Mr. Capone*, p. 318.

19. Ibid., p. 324.

20. *New York Times*, 15, 16, 17 March 1891.

21. For information on lynchings, see Luciano J. Iorizzo, *Italian Immigration and the Impact of the Padrone System* (New York, 1980), pp. 212–14.

Chapter 12

INCARCERATION

Capone's stay in Cook County Jail illuminated the dark side that passed for the justice system in Chicago. Putting Capone behind bars did not change anything. Speakeasies thrived. Bootlegging continued. Officials got their regular payoffs. Was the syndicate so strongly put together that it could withstand the removal of its leader? Was he only a figurehead? Capone biographer Laurence Bergreen claims the real Mr. Big was Frankie La Porte, from the nearby suburb of Chicago Heights. He made Capone cower. He was the mastermind who operated so effectively and so secretively that no one in authority knew of him. He gained in stature and power while law enforcement personnel expended virtually all their efforts to insure that they would bring Capone to justice. The implication is that officials went after the wrong man. Fighting the evils of Prohibition would have been better served by nailing La Porte.[1]

Bergreen's case is not a strong one. But whether or not La Porte was more powerful than Capone (which is highly unlikely), Bergreen misses the point. The essential problem was not any one person or syndicate. The central stumbling block was the corruption that was an integral part of American political life. Politicians, and the law enforcement personnel whom they controlled, realized that an accommodation had to be made with citizens in the enforcement of victimless crimes—offenses that citizens willingly committed to satisfy desires that were considered vices proscribed by law. Gambling and prostitution were long held in that regard. With the advent of Prohibition nationwide, a substantial number of Americans joined the chorus in asking for a policy of non-enforcement. The ideal of having a dry society became too impractical. It was unenforceable. There were simply too many people who had grown up in an atmosphere where alcoholic drinks were consumed as food and not thought of as demon rum. Mayor William Hale Thompson ran on a wide-open platform. He proudly stated that he was wetter than the Atlantic Ocean. He won the mayor's seat a number of times. As long as the public and its politicians held wet views, no amount of arresting and imprisoning bootleggers would stop Prohibition violations. There would always be an element ready to step in and take over. The rewards were great enough to run the risk of apprehension, conviction, and jail. In essence, until the public demanded a change in the system, the interrelationships between businessmen, public officials, and the criminal element would continue along their venal and corrupt ways.

Alas, for Al Capone, his glory days ended in May 1932. Federal marshals escorted him to the Dearborn train station. Atlanta Penitentiary was the ultimate destination. Fearing some wild attempt to free Capone before he entrained, Elliot Ness and his squad rode along to insure there would be no last-minute, highly dramatic escape. No such effort materialized. All along the roadside the curious public gathered to get a last glimpse of the Big Fellow, who was surrounded by reporters and law enforcement officers. Manacled to another prisoner and aware of many in the crowd who were happy to see him going to prison, he drew some consolation from the many well-wishers, family, and friends who came to see him off.

The train ride itself was depressing. He was accustomed to riding to Florida in grand style, sometimes even taking over a whole train in the process or partying with the best of wine, women, song, and good food. Not this time. The marshals controlled his every move. The monotony was broken occasionally when fellow passengers stopped by to wish him well and when he was able to wave to the throngs who had gathered along the way to catch a glimpse of the notorious gangster as the train slowed coming into small towns. Knowing that every step of his journey was being reported on the radio boosted his ego and helped soften the humiliating blows of being led away like a common criminal, which he never considered himself to be. In his own mind, he was a benefactor of Chicago, much better than the white-collar criminals who stole the people and the city blind and never gave back as he did to the poor, the homeless, and the countless victims of the Depression. Moreover, he was always quick to point out that he never attacked innocent people, which was something that bank robbers and stick-up artists could not say.

Capone arrived at Atlanta on May 4, 1932. He was looking at a sentence that would last to January 19, 1939, at the earliest and May 3, 1948, at the latest. He was identified as number 40886. Warden A.C. Aderhold ran a tight ship and did not tolerate the kinds of graft and corruption that at times flourished in federal and state prisons. Capone found out quickly that prison life in Atlanta would not be as easily manipulated as it was in Pennsylvania and Chicago.

Capone went through an indoctrination period at Atlanta that included interviews, quarantine, shots, and a complete physical including blood work. Before the results came back he began to exhibit symptoms of tertiary syphilis. Prison officials noticed that he acted strangely. Showing signs of a messianic complex, he claimed to be the savior of many of the downtrodden in Chicago by stepping in to fulfill the role that city government failed to do. Syphilis was the most serious of his health problems. But he also suffered from chronic prostatitis, probably attributable to gonorrhea. Later, at Alcatraz, a physician discovered that Capone had a "perforated nasal septum" which in all likelihood came from snorting cocaine from the early 1920s on.[2] Certainly Capone dealing in booze and brothels was in the thick of where the action was for cocaine. Any one of the above health problems would be enough to weigh heavily on an individual physically. When applied to an inmate of a hard-time federal penitentiary, the psychological impact made the burden all the more difficult.

Capone was only 33 years old when he entered Atlanta. But years of hard living had begun to take their toll on him. His attitude fluctuated widely. At times, he was a model prisoner acknowledging that he had a debt to pay society. He held no grudges against the people who put him there. For example, he knew that Elliot Ness was doing his job and he could respect an honest lawman. He owned up to authority in prison. He tried to be a good inmate. He worked in the shoe shop helping to repair shoes. Unable to write well, he busied himself by reading letters, newspapers, and sports magazines. Looking forward to an early release, he hired lawyers who were specialists in getting their clients off early.

It was not always easy for Capone to play by the rules of the game. Rumors circulated that he was buying his way through Atlanta, gaining favors from the warden and guards, having his regular supply of cocaine smuggled in. They were not true. But, believing the wild stories and seeing him as a warden's pet, many fellow prisoners had little respect for him. They made life miserable for him, threatened his life, tried to extort money from him. This bothered Capone to no end. So too, at times, he would complain bitterly about his attorneys, whom he felt were incompetent and not working hard enough to get him out of jail. He couldn't understand how he could pay them so well and have so little to show for it. He was losing sight of reality. No matter how hard his attorneys worked, no matter how many technicalities they could uncover, no judge was going to go down in history as the solon who freed Capone on a technicality.[3] His behavior became completely unpredictable when his syphilis would actively attack his central nervous system. At those times, he would have no control over his actions. Model prisoner could become raging lunatic.

It was Red Rudensky who helped Capone through these early years in prison. Born Max Motel Friedman in the lower East Side of New York, Rudensky had established himself as a master criminal by age 21. Starting out as a young punk doing small heists, he wound up in a state reformatory in Elmira, New York. There he learned the tools of the trade from old pros, who taught him the finer points of safe cracking and lock picking. He put his skills to use in Missouri, Michigan, Illinois, and Indiana, where he did jobs for Bugs Moran, the Purple Gang, Al Capone, and others. The underworld came to value him as one of the best at his trade. By the time he was caught in a failed jewelry robbery in St. Louis, he had earned as reputation for being one of the "smartest, youngest, and toughest" hoods in the country, responsible for pilfering many millions of dollars in cash and merchandise.[4] Undergoing a conversion in prison, Rudensky, defying a bloodthirsty mob, saved the life of Tom White, warden at Leavenworth. Rudensky was no one to fool with in prison. He had the respect of the most hardened inmates in whatever penitentiary he was. It was Capone's good fortune to become his cellmate.

Though nine years Capone's junior and certainly not in the same league as Capone in terms of leadership and national stature, Rudensky came to be the Big Guy's mentor and protector. As mentioned above, Capone's acceptance of his fate led other inmates to believe he was weak. It was the efforts of Rudensky that put an end to their harassment. He ordered the perpetrators to be roughed up. He then assigned some of his cohorts to act as bodyguards for Capone. It was just like the old days in Chicago. Wherever Scarface went, a contingent of Red's men were there to insure that no harm would befall him. Sharing a cell with Capone gave Rudensky a unique view of Capone. Red saw the family side of America's most feared bootlegger. He heard over and over how the Big Guy loved his wife, his mother, his son. He witnessed Capone going after letters from home like a lovesick and homesick soldier scrambling to make mail call. He detected a religious person, a doting father, a humble man who bore no ill will against those who sent him away. And he knew that something was not quite right with the Big Fellow. At times, not very often, Capone would go through sieges and fits, ranting and raving about his lawyers who were doing little or nothing to get him out. Rudensky had no way of

knowing that this behavior was due to physical and psychological abnor-
malities.

Capone and Rudensky were good for each other. Sharing a common
background of upbringing in New York City and a life of crime, they understood and trusted one another. They could entertain themselves with
radio shows, magazines, and newspapers and discuss matters of mutual interest. Like roommates in a college dormitory, they talked hopefully of the
day that they would go on to a better and brighter future. Red's dream
would come through. Capone's would turn into a nightmare.

It all started on August 19, 1934. Under conditions cloaked in secrecy
befitting a wartime maneuver and with no advance notice, 43 inmates left
Atlanta in an armored train. For security reasons they were manacled
hand and foot. Capone was among them. Their destination turned out to
be Alcatraz, designed to hold the country's most incorrigible prisoners and
destined to become America's most notorious and foreboding prison. Its
nicknames, "the Rock" and "Uncle Sam's Devil Island," put the fear of
God into all who were slated to do time there.

Sitting in beautiful San Francisco Bay, Alcatraz was named in 1775 by
Spanish explorers after the many pelicans that made their home on the island. It was uninhabited and mostly barren. In 1847, the United States
Army began to develop it as a fortress to protect the western reaches of
the nation. Heavily armored, it served its purpose until advances in military technology led to newer weaponry. Its natural isolation due to cold
surrounding water and unpredictably swift currents made it an ideal site
for a prison to house Civil War prisoners. It served the same purpose in
1898 during the Spanish-American War, and later housed civilian prisoners during the catastrophic earthquake that shook San Francisco in 1906.

From the start, though the government beautified the sterile grounds
somewhat, Alcatraz gained a reputation as a tough military prison. In
1934, beset by high operating costs, the military abandoned the site and
gave it over to the Department of Justice. The department immediately
set out to make it the home for roughly 300 of the nation's most difficult
inmates.

The Bureau of Prisons selected James A. Johnston as the first warden of
Alcatraz. An experienced penologist interested in reform, education, and
working inmates, Johnston's rule was marked by strict discipline, rigidity,
and harsh punishments. Courts did not sentence prisoners to the Rock.
They were sent from other federal prisons. No inmate would be accorded
special treatment. All would have limited privileges. Visitors were limited
to one per month upon approval of the warden. Access to radios, newspapers, and unapproved reading matter was not allowed. Incoming and out-

going mail was censored. All prisoners were expected to work as a privilege, not a right. Confined to one-person cells, the convicts were effectively isolated. These were highly restrictive living conditions, but harshest of all was the rule of silence imposed in the early years. The toughest hoods were known to crack, given their inability to socialize in any meaningful way. As if these imposed restrictions weren't enough of a burden, the site itself contributed to the mental torture. Prisoners were in earshot of the activity of pleasure craft, fishing vessels, ocean liners, automobiles, and aircraft, which they could also see as they passed through the waters, crossed the bridges, and flew overhead. There was constant traffic going to and from San Francisco, Oakland, and numerous communities in and around the harbor area. It served to further depress the inmates, who daily felt the enormous energy around them and could not be a part of it. Denied access to the media, they couldn't even understand what it was about.

The criteria for eligibility to this Devil Island were basically to be rated among the most troublesome and most likely to attempt escapes. Capone fit neither of those categories. But for an occasional outburst due to his medical condition, he might be considered an ideal prisoner. A third consideration, however, seemed to be made for him. High-profile convicts likely to receive special treatment were prime candidates for Alcatraz. Wardens in other facilities were able to rid themselves of people like Capone, who, if not actually receiving preferential treatment, were likely to give the media reason to speculate that they were. This would draw undue and unwanted attention to their institutions. Better to send inmates like that to Alcatraz and head off any public relations problems.

So it was that Capone was among the first inmates at Alcatraz. The reporters who had followed him, in the hopes of informing the nation of the continuing saga of Scarface, were allowed no closer than 200 yards offshore. He landed there with convicted kidnappers, bank robbers, and killers. They were all treated the same. None were greeted with any special recognition of their notoriety. Capone tried to glad-hand the warden but was summarily rebuffed. Johnston had set the tone for Capone's stay on the Rock. He would be known as number 85. The daily routine never changed. The cons would rise at 6:30 A.M. and answer to roll call. At 6:55 A.M. they would march single-file to breakfast. Johnston believed in feeding the men plenty so they had energy to work. At 7:15 A.M. they lined up for their assignments. Capone usually performed laundry chores, carried books back and forth from the library to cells, and swabbed the decks. Indicative of the anti-Italian prejudice in pre–World War II America and of the little respect the Big Fellow commanded, he became known as "the

Wop with the mop."[5] This was a huge comedown for the man who once believed, in a moment of delirium, that if the Irish mobsters in Chicago went along with him he could have been president of the United States.[6] With a ratio of one to three, guards were able to keep a tight rein on the prisoners. And so it went throughout the day, eating, marching, working, and standing for roll call time and time again. Occasionally, family visitors were allowed. Conjugal visits were unthinkable. As a matter of fact, no physical contact whatsoever was possible, since partitions with glass peepholes separated inmates from their loved ones. Private verbal communication was all but impossible, since any spoken word reached everyone in the cell house, easily cutting through the ambience of dead silence that permeated Alcatraz. It would be difficult to say who was more affected by such bittersweet visits, Al or his wife, Mae, and their young son, Sonny, who had to travel close to 3,000 miles to catch a glimpse of their husband and father.

The monotony was also broken by the formation of an inmates' band. Always around music in his speakeasies and a longtime fan of opera, Capone and some of his B Block mates relentlessly kept after Warden Johnston to allow a convict's band. Johnston finally gave in after a year. But it was a hollow victory for the cons. The band had up to 20 minutes a day to practice. This would hardly give each member time to tune up and warm up before the sessions were over. Having no previous musical experience with instruments, Capone chose the banjo and began to familiarize himself with notation and technique. He later switched to the mandolin, an instrument with which many an Italian immigrant plucked out Neapolitan love songs. After a while, he was able to play and sing some simple tunes. It was a short-lived experiment. Asking hardened individuals, who were accustomed to doing things their way, to blend harmoniously together, contributing here, being mute there, playing softly or loudly as the music required, was too much to expect. Capone eventually had to be content confining himself to playing and singing solo.[7]

Never able to win any special treatment from Johnston, Capone endured four and a half years of Alcatraz. Having no Red Rudensky to protect him, he survived on his own. In late 1935, a fellow band member clobbered Capone with a saxophone because Al had complained he was blowing it too loud near his ears. They came to blows and earned a week's isolation for the incident. Soon after, in January 1936, the inmates called a strike to protest the death of one of their own, Jack Allen. Allen's complaints of a stomach ailment had been ignored by prison officials until it was too late. Capone faced a serious dilemma. If he joined the strike he ran the risk of being identified as its leader. If he

refused, which he did, he opened himself to abuse from his fellow inmates. Not understanding or caring about his position, they tried to extort money from him and otherwise make life difficult for him. Some of
the more bloodthirsty among them decided to kill Capone. They went
after him with a pair of scissors. Seriously wounded, he was rushed to the
prison hospital. He survived and, after a short convalescence, was dis-
charged. The media turned the spotlight on Capone's ordeal. It reinforced tales of the ghastly regimen of Alcatraz, which more and more
people began to view as a sadistic, punishment-oriented institution
more likely to turn prisoners into madmen than inspire them to rehabil-
itate themselves. While Capone accepted his fate and showed no ten-
dency to want to get revenge on the system, the same could not be said
for the majority of inmates, whose hardened nature was made all the
worse for undergoing what many were beginning to view as cruel and
unusual punishment.[8]

In early February 1938, Capone became disoriented on his way to
breakfast. He didn't know where he was or what he was doing. He became
violently ill, as though an attack of stomach flu caused him to lose all it
contained. Rushed to the prison hospital, he soon realized that this was no
ordinary vomiting session. A prison doctor traced his problems to "paresis," a euphemism for syphilis, which was not yet a word used in polite society. Since being diagnosed with it in Atlanta, Capone had undergone
three treatments to battle the disease.[9] A press release told the world that
Capone was hospitalized and under observation, and that a definite diag-
nosis was yet to be determined. Mae Capone was beside herself. Her com-
muniqués to Johnston elicited vague replies that her husband would
remain in Alcatraz and receive good medical attention. A more extensive
physical examination of Capone revealed his damaged septum from continued use of cocaine in the 1920s. More serious, doctors discovered a
man who carried on conversations with God and His angels and unveiled
vague, grandiose plans to solve America's Depression. Capone exhibited
the classic symptoms of syphilis: the disablement of bones, muscle, and
nerve tissue. The prognosis was not good. Years of profligate living had
turned this 39-year-old into an old and sick man. His ailments were not
fatal in the short term. They did rob him, however, of his mental acuity.
He could no longer distinguish between fantasy and reality. Essentially, he
would never be able to function on his own.[10] Hospitalized, Capone would
remain incarcerated, but would never return to population—that is, he
would never mingle again with fellow inmates in the mess hall, recreation
area, the library, work areas, or wherever they were free to go when not in
their cells.

Fearful he would be accused of showing partiality to Capone, Johnston was reluctant to release him to another institution. Since his breakdown, Capone had been confined as a mentally unstable individual to a wire cage. Indeed, he was sick. But he was not violent. Nor was he dangerous. But the hospital had no provision for separating the mentally ill according to their inclination to be a threat to those around them. Just being hospitalized would have been a sufficient way to care for and contain Capone. But this was Alcatraz. There was only one approach to treating problems and that was the hardened one. When Capone got into a feces-throwing battle with another "crazy" (made possible since only wire, not a solid wall, separated them), the warden knew he had to act. On January 6, 1939, Johnston freed Capone from his cage[11] and sent him to the Federal Correctional Institution at Terminal Island, California, to complete his sentence. One year remained. Judge Wilkerson had required Capone to do his last year in Cook County. Federal officials persuaded the judge to agree to the California site. Capone stayed there until November. The government then sent him to Lewisberg Federal Penitentiary, where he would be released on November 16 under parole that would last until May 3, 1942.

Mae and Sonny saw a completely different man than the one who left them in 1931. Gone were the elegant, though somewhat gaudy clothes. There was no pearl gray fedora. No silk shirts. He looked like what he was, a convict being released from a long stretch of doing hard time. Try as he did to put on a good face, his mumbling, incoherent speech, his shuffling gait, and his inability to recall precisely what had happened to him for the last eight years told the sad story of a beaten man with a hopeless future. Capone, of course, didn't see it that way. He continued to speak in lucid moments of great accomplishments to come in the legitimate business world if not in the rackets. He and Mae and the rest of the family clung to the slim chance that a cure awaited him at Johns Hopkins Hospital in Baltimore, Maryland.

Doctors had been treating Capone for syphilis while he was in prison. But they had little success because they diagnosed the disease after it had progressed too far and because there was no easy cure for that venereal disease no matter when found out. Johns Hopkins had, perhaps, the foremost authority on syphilis in Dr. J. Earle Moore. In rare moments of awareness, Capone was intelligent enough to know that he needed help. He consented to be treated by Dr. Moore.

Dr. Moore ran into trouble at Johns Hopkins. The medical community there, in general, would have nothing to do with treating Al Capone, whom they considered unworthy of their time and attention. Dr. Moore moved him to Union Memorial Hospital where, backed by the medical board, he was able to overcome similar strenuous opposition. He began to administer the malaria treatment to his patient, theorizing that high fevers would eradicate the paralyzing spirochetes, the spiral-shaped organisms which carry the potentially deadly disease. Indeed, the high fevers did as expected. Such a treatment was effective in holding the line against further deterioration of the damage to the central nervous system. But, like patients who suffer from glaucoma today, doctors can only prevent further loss of sight, not restore that which has been lost. Capone's disease had done its damage. No amount of treatment could undo it. Still, Capone underwent treatments for four months. His health stabilized and he took off for his Florida home, arriving there on March 22, 1940.[12]

NOTES

1. Laurence Bergreen, *Capone: The Man and the Era* (New York, 1994), pp. 406, 499.

2. Ibid., p. 116.

3. Ibid., p. 516.

4. Robert Jay Nash, *Bloodletters and Badmen: A Narrative Encyclopedia of American Criminals from the Pilgrims to the Present* (New York, 1973), pp. 478–81.

5. Bergreen, *Capone: The Man*, p. 541. There is a wealth of information on Alcatraz and its history at www.alcatrazhistory.com, August 15, 2002.

6. Bergreen, *Capone: The Man*, p. 515.

7. Ibid., p. 549.

8. Ibid., pp. 549–52.

9. Ibid., pp. 559–80.

10. Ibid., p. 558.

11. Ibid., pp. 563–64.

12. Ibid., p. 581.

Chapter 13

PALM ISLE

Capone spent the last eight years of his life at his villa on Palm Isle with his extended family, which included Sonny; Mae; her sister, Muriel; and her husband, Louis Clark. They were attended by two servants who performed general household tasks. Coming in daily from their homes, they did the cooking, cleaning, and utility chores. Mae's brother, Dennis Coughlin, who went by the name of Danny, and his wife, Winifred, lived nearby and visited often. Coughlin acted as business agent for a local union and ran two businesses on the side with his wife. It's possible that they contributed to the support of Al and Mae. More likely, it was Ralph Capone who continued to provide the financial support from money gained from the rackets that Al had built up in the 1920s. This enabled Capone to live very comfortably, though nowhere near the level to which he had become accustomed in his halcyon days in Chicago. Even if Capone had continued to rake in millions while in retirement, his physical and mental condition precluded him from living life to the fullest. The verve, the dash, the swagger were gone. Capone had aged beyond his years. In his early 40s, his body resembled more a worn-out 50–60-year-old. His mind worked feebly at times. At other times, it could not deal with reason and reality. In effect, the Al Capone that people knew worldwide no longer existed. Yet life went on.

The daily routine kept the Capones busy. Mae frequently went to daily Mass. Though Capone was Catholic and was known to carry rosary beads, he belonged to that fraternity of Christians who, it was humorously said, attended services three times in their lives: when they were hatched, matched, and dispatched.[1] He did, however, witness Sonny's church wedding in December 1941. It is said that Capone stayed away from church services to avoid embarrassing the clergy and parishioners, who knew his gangster reputation all too well.

Capone kept busy. At one time an able fisherman who once caught, from his yacht, a sailfish measuring close to eight feet, he was reduced to going through the motions, simply dipping a rod into the water off his dock.[2] He played cards with his cronies, who visited him often. Fading in and out of reality, he still knew enough to figure out when someone beat him at gin rummy or pinochle. Out of respect for their former boss, they seldom did. If perchance they slipped up and won, Capone would "issue orders" to have his men take care of the "wise guys."[3] He enjoyed swatting a tennis ball across a makeshift grass court. In many ways Capone was living the life the way a white-collar criminal would do in federal institutions, which gained reputations as "country clubs" because of their easy-regimen approach to incarcerating "gentlemen" lawbreakers. Despite his fragile mental condition, or maybe because of it, the Big Guy didn't relish being alone. Yet he would trust only family members and cohorts he could remember from his glory days. It was his grandchildren and nieces and nephews who gave Capone his happiest moments. Sonny's wife produced four girls. Capone doted on them. He gave them expensive presents and played with them endlessly in the family pool. And then there was the unexpected family who thrilled Capone no end.

It was in 1941, when Al, visiting his brother Ralph at a family hideaway in Wisconsin, reunited with his oldest brother Vincenzo, better known as Richard James "Two Gun" Hart. Hart had set out on his own at an early age. Leaving Brooklyn, he went west. Part con man and part hero, he married, settled down, and managed to hide the fact that he was related to Al Capone. Ironically, Hart made a name for himself fighting as a lawman who specialized in uncovering liquor sales to Indian tribes in the Midwest. Falling upon hard times, Hart contacted his brothers, who, through Ralph, helped him and his family get through the difficult Depression days. Hart took three of his young boys on his "family reunion." They met their uncle Al for the first time and came to idolize him. They spent many hours together, usually roughhousing. Al loved it. So did the youngsters, especially when he showered them with hundred-dollar bills.[4] Except for memory lapses, neither Hart nor his sons could detect any serious health problems in Capone. And those symptoms were glossed over as being due to his incarceration in Alcatraz. They missed the reality of the situation. Jake Guzik got to the heart of the matter. Knowing that Guzik had visited with Capone, reporters in Chicago asked him if Capone would return to the rackets there. Guzik said, "Al is nutty as a fruitcake."[5]

In 1942, doctors included Al Capone among the first syphilitics to be treated with penicillin. In doing so, they probably prolonged his life, or at least made it somewhat tolerable. But they could not reverse the damage. Eventually, Capone's body gave out. He died on January 25, 1947.

NOTES

1. This humorous description has been told by many scholars, but the author first heard it from the late Monsignor Gannon Ryan, Chaplain, Syracuse University, on September 28, 1960.

2. Robert J. Schoenberg, Mr. *Capone* (New York, 2001), p. 266.

3. John K. Kobler, *Capone: The Life and World of Al Capone* (New York, 1971), p. 383.

4. Laurence Bergreen, *Capone: The Man and the Era* (New York, 1994), p. 592.

5. Kobler, *Capone*, p. 381.

Chapter 14

FINAL THOUGHTS ON CAPONE

Capone lives on for a multitude of reasons. Overall, from the 1920s to the present, people have been writing books and articles about him, making movies, and taping television features. But there is no definitive work, no closure on Capone, as it were, by which people can put his story to rest. The print media, highly critical of Capone during his heyday, has become more balanced, even sympathetic at times, given to probing deeply into the complicated world of Prohibition, the role of gangs, and the emergence of modern organized crime. Subjects such as the role of alliances between criminals and politicians in running America's governments at all levels, which have scarcely been touched upon in traditional academic circles, are now coming to the fore and drawing an ever-broader audience in colleges and universities, and among the general public. This adds up to renewed interest in major figures like Al Capone. Hollywood and television generally continue to present the stereotypical view focusing on the violence and brutality associated with Capone and his era. They feed the curious with blood and guts, commodities that the public can't seem to get enough of regardless of who is the principal subject.

Specifically, Capone was a very popular personality who has become synonymous with Chicago, Prohibition, and the Roaring Twenties. It is difficult to speak of the Windy City and/or those events without Capone's name popping up. The media reported his doings for all the world to know. He became, or it made of him, a folk hero alongside Jesse James. America's preoccupation with the Mafia has also translated into popular appeal for Capone. Though he never was a mafioso, the erroneous equating of organized crime with the Mafia and Italian American criminals has made an indelible mark in the minds of Americans, which serves to lead them to automatically identify high-profile criminals such as Capone with the Mafia.

Beyond that, Capone did things that some people wish they had the guts to do at one time or another. He fearlessly put his life on the line. He was dangerously daring. He resisted authority, broke laws that he felt were senseless, and tried to avoid paying income taxes. He stood up to rival gangsters when he felt they broke their word to him and eliminated those close to him who, he had good reason to believe, either betrayed or were about to betray him. He lashed out at what he considered inequities in life, trying to set them straight, be it assisting people to gain honest employment or helping them fend off extortionists. He fought city hall and got to "own" it for a while. He gave generously to the needy and lifted the spirits of the downtrodden. He was an equal-opportunity employer before the government made it politically correct and legally binding to do so. He led a glamorous and exciting life. He tooled around town in luxurious automobiles, accompanied by a fleet of cars ahead and behind him manned by bodyguards at the ready to serve and protect him. One of those was a custom-built 1930 V-16 Cadillac, which had a top speed of 120 miles per hour, bulletproof glass, one-quarter-inch armor plate lining on the driver's side, and three-inch portholes in the side windows that could be used to fire machine guns at any attackers. The gas tank was bulletproof and a tube protruded through the floorboard so that nails could be dropped on the highway to slow down pursuers. If all of that failed, a device could be activated that created a smoke screen through the exhaust system, which caused the drivers behind them to lose sight of where they were going. Capone, it was believed, paid $20,000 for the automobile, which was a considerable sum of money to pay for a car in the 1920s. When he felt unthreatened he would ride in his sporty 1925 six-cylinder four-door Packard convertible, which seated five. It was recently pictured on the Internet and offered for sale for $49,900.[1]

Before airplanes became the preferred way of travel, he used them. He rode ostentatiously in the best trains of the day. He fulfilled his American dream of becoming a multimillionaire, a living example that one could rise from humble beginnings to untold riches, before he turned 30 years old. His wardrobe was of the highest quality, flamboyantly colorful, outrageously expensive, and complemented with an assortment of diamonds that dazzled onlookers. Capone had the status symbols befitting the wealthiest financiers and businessmen: cars, boats, an island home on the Bay of Biscayne, celebrities willing to befriend him, people from the right side of the law eager to socialize with him for the sake of being able to tell others in their circle that they had met and rubbed elbows with Al Capone. And he played golf when it was still a pastime that appealed mostly to the rich.

Despite all the outward signs of vanity, he was generous to a fault. He tipped lavishly, donated handsome sums to charities, fed some of the poor during the Depression, and had a disdain for money, which he felt was useless unless it was spent. This was said to be a source of his power, for his men shared generously in the profits of his undertakings. He was a genuine spendthrift and many people loved him for being one. He often gave his friends and acquaintances diamond jewelry and money. He was known to lose hundreds of thousands of dollars during a racing season, which pleased his bookies no end. If he had an ulterior motive in dispensing money freely, it could be that he felt that his generosity would help him maintain his leadership status, atone for his criminal actions, and motivate people to accept him for what he yearned to be known as: a businessman just giving the public what they craved. Perhaps the public could be made to forget, or at least put to the back of their minds, the St. Valentine's Day massacre, which he is credited with engineering, and the incredibly brutal, fatal battering that he was said to have administered personally to Anselmi, Scalise, and Guinta, traitors to his cause. The press had covered those killings in great detail, photos included, as well as many other criminal acts that it credited to Capone.

Capone's bravado appealed to the average American as well as to the most successful sports figures, politicians, opera stars, entertainers, sportswriters, authors, and many others. He was an ingratiating personality who threw people off guard by treating them in such a gentlemanly and classy manner that he could make them minimize the effect of the ugly things they had read about him in the newspapers. He didn't talk like a gangster. Capone in person did not exhibit the characteristics of the cagey, crafty, cold-blooded killer they had read about and expected to witness.

Despite the many beastly criminal acts charged to Capone, many people, especially youngsters, admired him, and a few even defended him. Among those who spoke on his behalf was Roland Libonati. Libonati was an attorney who had been a U.S. Army officer in World War I and represented a district in Chicago for 16 years in the U.S. House of Representatives.[2] Libonati did not necessarily condone the crimes Capone committed. He preferred to view Capone's uses of violence as acts of self-defense. Libonati gave Capone credit for achieving enormous results against great odds, especially crediting Capone with becoming a hero in the eyes of many Italian Americans for getting rid of Italian criminals who preyed upon their own kind. Apparently, Capone's apologia had some positive effect on his reputation with people like Libonati. Not so with Tony Berardi, the newspaper photographer, another contemporary of Capone. Having taken pictures of a number of Capone's alleged victims, Berardi felt he knew, firsthand, of Capone's ruthless nature. Reflecting an overwhelming view held by Italian Americans today, he believed Capone to be a detriment to them, reinforcing the stereotype of Italian American criminality that has continued into the twenty-first century. Yet, strange as it seems, Berardi enjoyed being around Capone and taking his picture.[3] If Berardi's repulsion/attraction for Capone does not explain Capone's good/evil nature, it should help us to understand what an enigmatic figure Capone is. And therein lies a major source of his continued allure.

Capone's detractors, who have been in an overwhelming majority over the years, point to his evil deeds, principally murdering, doing drugs, peddling illegal alcohol, fostering prostitution, bribing public officials, and failing to pay his income tax. While the print media, as stated, has tempered that treatment of Capone, the visuals, which continue to feed the Capone mystique, stress that dark side of him. Some comments on a few of the more noteworthy and relevant Hollywood films and videos will demonstrate that point.

Hollywood has been keeping Capone in the public eye for over 70 years. Television has been doing its part for close to five decades. With a background of Italian American criminality dating from the 1880s, with first the Mafia and then the Black Hand scares in Chicago, Capone captured the attention of Americans so thoroughly that they began to view Italian Americans as the preeminent criminals in the country, taking the place of the Irish, who up until then were cast as the major villains in motion pictures, reflecting the reality of Irish criminal activity in urban America. With the appearance of the film *Little Caesar* in 1930, focusing on a fictional Italian American criminal, Rico Bandello, Capone became the model for a number of Hollywood movies featuring violence, corruption, and gangsters with Italian names. *Scarface* in 1932 reinforced the emergence of the Italian American gangsters as the kingpins of crime and established Capone as the chief among them. The film set the tone for countless gangster films to come. The more they focused on the Capone model, the less they dealt with the public's and the public officials' flagging responsibility to maintain law and order. These gangster films, which proliferated up to the twenty-first century, essentially portrayed Capone's madness, violence, ruthlessness, and his profligate lifestyle filled with gambling, drinking, and womanizing. Loosely based on the folklore of

Capone rather than any solid scholarship, they are mostly fiction, utilizing outright inventions designed to appeal to the public's thirst for gross entertainment and titillation. A sample of the films is listed in the bibliography.

Television fares only somewhat better than Hollywood in that TV attempts to present a more accurate account of Capone by sometimes using the bio-historical approach. Many of Capone's biographers are interviewed in *Biography* (1997). They lend a revisionist, somewhat sympathetic tone to Capone's life. They talk of his generosity and concern for the downtrodden and tend to soften the harsh criminal side otherwise shown. But the audiovisual message of bombs bursting, bullets flying, buildings engulfed in flames, and bodies dropping stays with the viewer long after any words.

Perhaps the most telling fact helping to explain the public's attraction to Capone is the existence of a Chicago bus tour that traces the various venues made famous (or infamous) by the Big Guy. It is testimony to the power of Capone to continue to attract the public's attention and to the ability of the media and the entertainment industry to thrive on the Capone mystique and push it to the limit.

The tour raises greater questions. Would Capone disappear if hucksters turned away from him? If they did so, would people demand to continue to learn about him? Would they try to solve the puzzle of how a murderer can be a loving family man? How a person with such an ingratiating smile can ruthlessly kill? Would Capone's animal magnetism still draw people to him? Would his unthinkable daring and raw ability, which brought him enormous economic success, keep dazzling people? Most likely, the public will still seek Capone's story because they are seduced by the Hollywood version of his life and charm.

Though the comics are no longer a major source of Capone's folklore, they were once a major factor in keeping Capone's name before the public. When Chester Gould's *Dick Tracy* made its debut in 1931, it featured as the antagonist Big Boy, a fat, cigar-smoking hood sketched to resemble Al Capone. Big Boy orders his boys to steal the life savings of Emil Trueheart, owner of a neighborhood delicatessen and father of Tracy's sweetheart, Tess. When Trueheart resists the intruders, they kill him and make off with his daughter. Thus was born the famous detective sworn to wage unrelenting war against racketeers who were either deformed or Italian Americans. Though he was sensitive to helping improve their status, Capone unwittingly played no small role in the formation of the caricature of Italian Americans as incorrigible gangsters. *Dick Tracy* served as a model for other popular superheroes like

Batman, Captain Marvel, and others who often fought Italian American extortionists and racketeers.[4]

By the early 1940s, the comic book superheroes had mopped up Italian American outlaws handily and had shown them to be inflated bullies. Art was imitating life. The Capone era of the 1920s and 1930s, which glamorized the negative image of Italian Americans, had come to an end. In the 1940s, Capone was wasting away in Florida, a shell of the once seemingly invincible king of crime. But he would not be forgotten. He continued to be the subject of numerous media projects (as the sample items in the bibliography demonstrate), though more and more the Mafia, *The Godfather*, La Cosa Nostra, and, lately, *The Sopranos* have taken precedence for the time being.

The net effect of the media, despite its emphasis on Capone's murderous and wayward ways, has been to lionize him. He has been called the most famous American in the world, has been likened to an emperor, and noted for his imposing size, smartness, and charm. Capone has become a legend, a folk hero, a staple in the nation's criminal history.

In sum, Capone was a complex man, an enigma. A man of enormous physical strength and practical intelligence, he chose to take the quick road to fame and fortune. He loved his wife, mother, siblings, and extended family. He showed this in many ways, taking care of their daily needs and furnishing them with the luxuries of life. He cared for the underdogs and generously provided for them on numerous occasions. He cautioned friends and neighbors not to follow his lifestyle.

In many ways, he had a deep respect for authority, which he demonstrated by trying to be a model prisoner. His docile behavior behind bars was also an indication of his religiosity, a silent admission of his wrongdoing, and an atonement for his corrupt behavior. A Roman Catholic, he explained away his lack of churchgoing by claiming his absence saved it from embarrassment.

Capone did honestly believe that he did nothing wrong in violating Prohibition laws. In an age where the establishment tried to eliminate drinking and minimize gambling and prostitution, he became a hero of sorts, making it possible for the common individual to partake of fruit that, though forbidden in his day and age, had been legally available throughout the nation's history. Capone knew that and capitalized on it.

Deep down, however, he knew that no matter how much his enemies deserved to die, he had to assume some responsibility and guilt for their executions. He could rationalize his gangster life because he understood that corruption was part and parcel of life in urban America. He could justify his actions because the law of the jungle said to do it to someone before that someone does it to you. That's the way the wise guys understood life to be. But Capone realized that the average American didn't view it that way. Capone saw that the media had marked him as a pariah in society, a brutal killer, a heartless villain, a profligate gambler, pimp, and racketeer. So he worked on his public relations, he smiled, put up a gregarious front, and worked his apologia every chance he got. Society finally put him away but never really rid itself of him.

Only time will tell how long the public will continue to be interested in Capone. As long as they demand books, movies, videos, and information on the Internet, media moguls will continue to supply them. Given the current demand for such material on Capone, the Big Guy should live on and on for many generations.

NOTES

1. An undated broadside from the Imperial Palace Hotel and Casino, Las Vegas, Nevada, has a description and picture of the 1930 Cadillac. This automobile is believed to be the one described in "Al Capone's Armoured [sic] Car," a memoir by Russell T. Barnhart on www.talesofold china.com/shanghai/t-capo.html, August 15, 2002. A description and two pictures of the 1925 Packard can be seen at http://www.miles-pocket watches.com/ 1925_Packard.html, August 15, 2002.

2. Martin Short, *Crime Inc.: The Story of Organized Crime* (London, 1984), pp. 84–87.

3. Ibid., p. 87.

4. Luciano J. Iorizzo and Salvatore Mondello, *The Italian Americans*, rev. ed. (Boston, 1980), pp. 263–84.

GLOSSARY OF NAMES
AND EVENTS

Aderhold, Warden A. C.
Warden of the U.S. Penitentiary at Atlanta.
Adonis, Joe (1902–1972)
Brooklyn gang leader.
Ahern, Michael J.
One of Capone's attorneys at his income tax trial.
Aiello, Joseph (1891–1930)
Minor North Side leader. He joined with Capone's enemies because of Capone's support of Tony Lombardo for president of the *Unione Siciliana* and offered $50,000 to anyone who would kill Capone.
Alcatraz
Federal penitentiary in San Francisco Bay, harboring the most hardened criminals. It housed Capone from August 22, 1934, to January 6, 1939.
Annenberg, Moses L. "Moe" (1877–1942)
Chicago newspaperman who monopolized the wire services and controlled various racing newspapers throughout the country. He attended the Atlantic City Conference and was considered, by some, a peer of the most powerful racketeers in the nation.
Anselmi, Albert (d. 1929)
See Guinta, Giuseppe "Hop Toad."
Atlanta Federal Penitentiary
Held Capone from May 4, 1932, to August 19, 1934.
Atlantic City Conference
Meeting in May 1929 of many top criminals who made strategic decisions, including the establishment of a national organized crime system,

setting up machinery for lay-off bets, tying the national wire service to the racing newspapers, and taking the heat off the underworld by having Capone get himself arrested and sent up for a minor charge in Philadelphia.

Becker, Charles (1869–1915)

New York City police lieutenant executed in Sing Sing for murder.

Bernstein, Abe

A major leader of the Purple Gang.

Black Hand

Groups of extortionists who preyed upon fellow immigrants in early part of the twentieth century.

Boat race

A fixed horse race.

Buchalter, Louis "Lepke" (1897–1944)

A leader of Murder, Inc. He was executed by the state.

Burke, Fred R. "Killer" (1893–ca. 1940)

Former member of St. Louis's Egan's Rats gang who joined Capone's gang and was believed to be a principal machine gunner in the St. Valentine's Day massacre.

Capone, Albert Francis "Sonny" (b. 1918)

Son of Capone and Mae Coughlin.

Capone, Raffaele "Ralph" (1894–1974)

One of Capone's older brothers and his right-hand man who specialized in prostitution and handled Al's business when he was away or incarcerated.

Capone, Salvatore "Frank" (1895–1924)

One of Capone's older brothers. He had a promising career in crime following in the Torrio mold, and was killed in Cicero.

Capone, Vincenzo "James" (1892–1951)

One of Capone's older brothers. He left the family at a very early age and built a career in law enforcement under the name Richard Joseph "Two Gun" Hart.

Clark, Louis

Married Muriel Coughlin, Mae Coughlin's sister.

Cleveland Conference

Meeting in December 1928 that laid groundwork for the Atlantic City Conference.

Colosimo, James "Big Jim" (1877–1920)

First Italian American syndicate leader in Chicago; he gave start to Torrio and Capone.

The Combination

Another name for syndicate, organized crime, etc.

Costello, Frank (1893–1973)
Peer of Lucky Luciano in the New York mob.
Coughlin, Dennis "Danny"
Brother-in-law of Capone.
Coughlin, John "Bathhouse"
First Ward alderman and political boss in Chicago who helped Colosimo's ascent from laborer to syndicate boss and made possible the rise of the Torrio-Capone gang.
Coughlin, Mary Josephine "Mae" (1897–1986)
Married Capone on December 30, 1918.
Coughlin, Muriel
Mae Coughlin's sister. Married Louis Clark.
D'Andrea, Anthony (d. 1921)
Political/criminal figure who helped corrupt the benevolent *Unione Siciliana* in Chicago.
D'Andrea, Phil
Capone's main bodyguard and a president of the *Unione Siciliana*.
Demora, James Vincenzo
See McGurn, "Machine Gun" Jack.
Dever, William E.
Reform mayor of Chicago from 1923 to 1927.
Drucci, Vincent "The Schemer" (1885–1927)
O'Banion gang member.
Druggan-Lake Gang
Terry Druggan and Frankie Lake's gang, the only Irish gang that consistently supported Capone. They controlled the West Side between Little Italy and Cicero.
Drys
Those who supported Prohibition and wanted it strictly enforced.
Fink, Albert
One of Capone's two major attorneys defending him in the income tax trial.
Five Points Gang
Controlled New York City's lower East Side and had satellite groups. It served as the proving ground for the likes of Johnny Torrio, Lucky Luciano, Frankie Yale, and Capone.
Flegenheimer, Arthur
See Schultz, Dutch.
Fotre, John
Western Union manager at Lexington Hotel who testified in Capone's income tax trial.

The Four Deuces

Torrio's four-story headquarters in Chicago, housing a saloon, a gambling den, and a brothel. Capone got his start in Chicago working there.

Genna Brothers

Angelo, Antonio, Mike, Pete, Sam, and Vincenzo "Jim" came from Marsala, Sicily. They set up an alky cooking empire in Chicago's Little Italy; their principal customer was Capone, who protected them from the Moran gang. In an effort to control the *Unione Siciliana*, they turned on Capone, only to be betrayed by Anselmi and Scalise.

Gig

Musician's talk, meaning a job.

Guinta, Giuseppe "Hop Toad" (d. 1929)

Capone gang member and a president of the *Unione Siciliana*. He was killed on May 7, 1929, for his role in the plot (with Anselmi and Scalise) to murder his boss.

Guzik, Jake (1886–1956)

Also called Jack. He and his brother Harry were members of Capone's gang. Jake went from whoremaster to Capone's chief economic advisor. Next to family, Guzik was the most trusted and closest aide to Capone.

Hart, Richard C. "Two Gun" (1892–1952)

See Capone, Vincenzo.

The Harvard Inn

Frankie Yale's bar in Coney Island, which gave Capone a start in the rackets.

Hawthorne Inn

Capone's headquarters in Cicero.

Hawthorne Kennel Club

Dog racing track in Cicero.

Hawthorne Smoke Shop

The first gambling house in Cicero run by Torrio and Capone.

Henderson Jr., Parker

Influential son of the late mayor of Miami who helped Capone establish himself in the Miami area.

Howard, Joseph (1896–1924)

Allegedly shot by Capone for manhandling Jake Guzik.

Humphreys, Murray "The Camel"

Hit man for Capone who rose to the board of directors of the Chicago mob.

Hunt, Samuel McPherson "Golf Bag"

Hit man for Capone who served as a pallbearer at Capone's funeral.

Irey, Elmer
Head of the Internal Revenue Service's Special Intelligence Unit, which began and pressed the investigation of Capone's income tax evasion.

Johnson, George E. Q.
Incorruptible U.S. Attorney for Chicago who came from WASP and rural roots; he prosecuted Capone for income tax evasion.

Johnston, Warden James A.
Warden of Alcatraz.

Kenna, Michael "Hinky Dink"
First Ward alderman and political boss in Chicago, who, with John "Bathhouse" Coughlin, gave protection to Colosimo and helped the rise to power of the Torrio-Capone gang.

Koncil, Frank "Lefty" (d. 1927)
Chauffeur for Joseph Saltis.

La Cosa Nostra
Term popularized by Joe Valachi to describe Italian American crime groups in the 1930s and interpreted to mean the Mafia, though Valachi never used that word. It served to make Italian Americans synonymous with organized crime and vice-versa.

Lansky, Meyer (1902–1983)
Leader in the push to Americanize organized crime utilizing the best talent regardless of ethnicity. Focused primarily on extending the syndicate's gambling operations internationally, he was particularly effective in bringing together Jewish and Italian gangsters. His chief partner was Lucky Luciano.

La Porte, Frankie
Chicago Heights gangster purported to be, by a few people, the man behind Capone.

Lay-off bets
System whereby bookmakers who get more business than they can handle or want to handle can pass on a portion of their action to a bookmaker's bookie.

Lepito, Michael
See Malone, Michael F.

Lewisburg Federal Penitentiary
Pennsylvania prison that was the site of Capone's release.

Lexington Hotel
One of Capone's headquarters in Chicago.

Lombardo, Antonio "Tony"
Capone's friend, a legitimate businessman connected to politicians and gangsters, who won presidency of the *Unione Siciliana* with Capone's support after Angelo Genna's murder.

Luciano, Charles "Lucky" (1897–1962)
Leader in getting Italian gangsters to get away from regional ties and integrate among themselves and with non-Italians; he helped to bring about a working relationship among gangs throughout the country under his leadership and that of his chief partner, Meyer Lansky.
Mafia
Western Sicilian secret organization of loosely tied groups in each community, originally established to mete out justice in place of foreign rulers; deeply embedded in society, it turned criminal. Some of its members emigrated to other countries but were not able to transplant an organization that was built and thrived on hundreds of years of infiltration into every aspect of Sicilian life. The Americanization of gangsters killed whatever chance mafiosi might have had of establishing their secret society in a new environment.
Malone, Michael F.
Frank Wilson's undercover agent who, under the name Michael Lepito, infiltrated the Capone gang.
Maranzano, Salvatore (1868–1931)
Highly educated Mafia boss from Castellammarese, Sicily, forced to leave Italy by the crackdown on criminals after Mussolini came to power; he tried to maintain a tight-knit closed Sicilian criminal group in New York City with himself as the "Boss of Bosses" when he immigrated to New York in 1927. He ordered the extermination of his reigning rival Joe "The Boss" Masseria, then was ordered killed by forces for integration of the mob led by Lucky Luciano, Bugsy Siegel, and Meyer Lansky.
Masseria, Giuseppe Joe "The Boss" (d. 1931)
Rival of Salvatore Maranzano for control of Italian American criminal groups, which he believed should not include outsiders (that is, non-Italians).
Mattingly, Lawrence P.
Capone's attorney who produced a letter on Capone's financial condition that detailed an estimate of Capone's income from 1926–29, which proved to be a key element in his income tax evasion trial and conviction.
McDonald, Michael Cassius
Of Chicago; he was an early model for the modern organized crime chieftains.
McGurn, "Machine Gun" Jack (1904–1936)
Hit man for Capone and principal suspect in the St. Valentine's Day killings. Formerly James Vincenzo De Mora.
McSwiggin, William
Assistant state's attorney, killed in gang shooting.
Metropole Hotel
One of Capone's headquarters in Chicago.

Moneypenny, Warden David
Warden of Cook County Jail.

Moore, Dr. J. Earle
Specialist in general paresis at Johns Hopkins Hospital who treated Capone.

Moran, George "Bugs" (1893–1957)
Of Polish/Irish parents, a member of the O'Banion-Weiss gang who eventually took over after their deaths.

Morrissey, John
Of New York; he was another early model for the modern organized crime chieftains.

Mutual Benefit Societies (MBS)
Also known as Mutual Aid Societies. These were benevolent organizations formed by immigrants, usually on the basis of origins in the old country, which provided for insurance benefits to its members in the days before the federal government established Social Security, unemployment insurance, worker's compensation, etc. Each Italian community, for example, had many of these societies; in the early twentieth century Chicago had about 400 such organizations and New York City about 2,000. Over the years, as the regionalism of immigrants waned and the number of immigrants began to diminish greatly, many of these societies merged. MBSs paid many death benefits to survivors of its members, which helped them pay burial costs and ease them through hard times.

Nash, Thomas D.
One-half of the highly ranked defense team (with Michael Ahern) who represented Capone.

National Crime Syndicate
An alternative name and more accurate description of organized crime in America than the popular term Mafia.

National Wire Service
Provided sports betting information by telephone and telegraph to bookmakers across the country.

Ness, Elliot
Put together a team of honest federal Prohibition agents in Chicago that came to be known as "the Untouchables."

Nitti, Frank "The Enforcer" (1884–1943)
Hit man who took over for Capone in 1930s.

O'Banion, Dion (1892–1924)
Leader of one of Chicago's most feared gangs and chief rival of the Torrio-Capone outfit.

O'Donnell Brothers, South Side

Edward "Spike," Steve, Walter, and Tommy; the brothers got along well with Torrio-Capone until Spike got out of prison in the summer of 1923, when they began encroaching on Torrio-Capone's territory and were eventually run out of business by the Saltis-McErlane gang, who at the time supported Capone and killed and wounded a number of O'Donnell gang members.

O'Donnell Brothers, West Side

William "Klondike," Bernard, and Miles; this was an all Irish gang allied at first with Torrio-Capone, then switched over to Moran. They decided to exit the wars after the triple killing involving McSwiggin.

O'Hare, Edward H.

Son of Edward J. O'Hare; he won the Congressional Medal of Honor for downing five Japanese bombers in World War II. Later killed in aerial combat, he was awarded the Congressional Medal of Honor and had Chicago's airport named after him.

O'Hare, Edward J.

Questionable attorney/businessman (and partner at times with Capone) who, as an informant, played a key role in the government's getting a conviction of Capone; he was shotgunned to death in his car.

Olds, Ransom E.

Builder of the Oldsmobile automobile; he had a cabin cruiser built which Capone eventually owned.

One-way Ride

An expression used to describe a method gangsters used to dispose undesirables: the victim would be driven to a remote site, murdered, and dumped. It gained currency with the advent of Prohibition and the automobile.

The Outfit

Another name for syndicate, National Crime Syndicate, or any other designation having to do with a nationally oriented organized crime group.

Population

Term used to describe those prisoners, who make up the vast majority of those incarcerated, who are free to mingle within the walls of a penitentiary, as opposed to those who are kept in isolation (that is, confined alone and prohibited from mingling with others).

Prohibition

Created by the Eighteenth Amendment to the U.S. Constitution; it forbade the manufacture, transportation, and sale of alcoholic liquors for beverage purposes and was enforced according to the provisions of the Volstead Act.

The Purple Gang

Detroit gang that was strategically placed to supply Canadian liquor to Chicago, mainly to Capone; it later partnered with the National Crime Syndicate of Lucky Luciano, Meyer Lansky, Lepke Buchalter, and others. Abe Bernstein was a major leader.

Racketeer

One who obtains money illegally by bootlegging, fraud, violence, and dishonest schemes and practices; some employ the term generally to refer to any easy way of making money.

Ricca, Paul "The Waiter" (1897–1972)

Brainy leader in Chicago with Frank Nitti, who supplied the brawn; Tony Accardo; and others. After Capone's imprisonment, Lucky Luciano and Meyer Lansky highly respected Ricca.

Ries, Fred

Capone's cashier, who many say was coerced to testify against Capone at his income tax trial.

Rio, Frank

Loyal bodyguard who uncovered the plot to kill Capone by Guinta, Anselmi, and Scalise.

Robber Barons

Buccaneers of industry charged with running roughshod over their rivals and exploiting America's resources, workers, and people in their headlong quest for monopolies and profit in the nineteenth century.

Rothstein, Arnold (1882–1928)

Gambling genius whose lay-off betting system fueled the development of the National Crime Syndicate; he was most influential gangster in New York City during the 1910s and 1920s, taking under his wing the likes of Lucky Luciano and Meyer Lansky.

Rudensky, Morris "Red" (b. 1908)

Master thief and Capone's cellmate in Atlanta; Red had freelanced for Capone as well as for the Purple Gang in Detroit and befriended Capone in prison.

Saltis-McErlane Gang

Joseph "Polack Joe" Saltis and Frank McErlane's gang on the South West Side of Chicago; they supported Capone, then worked with Weiss against their former cohort; they later warred with the Sheldons (Capone's ally); McErlane quit in 1929, Saltis in 1930; Capone absorbed their territory.

Scalise, John (d. 1929)

See Guinta.

Schultz, Dutch (1902–1935)

Gangster who reportedly challenged Capone's move into the National Crime Syndicate. Formerly Arthur Flegenheimer.

Sheldon Gang

Led by Ralph Sheldon, principally pro-Capone though sometimes buying from Moran. The gang dispersed early in the 1930s with the establishment of the National Crime Syndicate.

The Ship

Gambling establishment Capone owned in partnership with Torrio and O'Banion.

Shumway, Leslie

Capone's bookkeeper at the Ship and the Hawthorne Smoke Shop who many say was coerced to testify against Capone at his income tax trial.

Siegel, Benjamin "Bugsy" (1906–1947)

Major mob member of the National Crime Syndicate, influential in its role of helping to develop gambling as a national attraction in Las Vegas.

Small, Governor Len

Governor of Illinois, a corrupt politician indebted to Torrio, Capone, and others, who pardoned whoremaster Harry Guzik among others for a price.

Stenson, Joseph

Member of the Stenson family in Chicago, which ran legitimate breweries; when Prohibition came he threw in with bootleggers and worked closely with Torrio-Capone, Druggan-Lake, and others.

St. Valentine's Day Massacre

Mass killings on February 14, 1929, that pushed the federal government to get Capone at any cost and led to his loss of popular support.

The Syndicate

Organized criminal association that emphasizes the economic (making money) rather than the social (forming groups based on race or ethnicity). Capone picked this word up from newspapers and used it to describe his mob. The word is often used as a synonym for the National Crime Syndicate, the Outfit, organized crime, the Mafia, La Cosa Nostra, the Combination, and so on.

Tennes, Mont (1865–1941)

Protégé of Mike McDonald and head of Chicago's premier gambling syndicate controlling the wire service nationwide; he retired in 1924 when the reform movement took over in Chicago and sold out to Moses Annenberg (50 percent) and others, including relatives.

Terminal Island
Federal correctional institution near Los Angeles, California, where Capone spent time after his release from Alcatraz and prior to his parole from Lewisburg Federal Penitentiary.

Thompson, William Hale
Mayor of Chicago who stood for a wide-open city.

Torrio, Johnny (1882–1957)
Mentor of Capone and a major architect of modern organized crime; he used force when necessary but mainly preached peaceful aggression through patience and business methods, and was an advisor to the likes of Lucky Luciano, Meyer Lansky, and others.

Unione Siciliana
Originally a benevolent mutual benefit society whose loose national ties made it an inviting target for gangsters to control and use for criminal purposes; the Chicago gangster Anthony D'Andrea took it over before Prohibition and by the mid-1920s the name *Unione Siciliana* was used to identify the Mafia in New York.

Untouchables
The name given to Elliot Ness's crew fighting Prohibition violations.

Valachi, Joseph (1904–1971)
Gang member/informant responsible for introducing the name *La Cosa Nostra*, which described Italian American crime groups in the 1930s; law enforcement personnel interpreted it to mean the Mafia, though Valachi never used that word. In essence, it made possible the selling of the Mafia as the organization responsible for organized crime in America. The U.S. government and the public viewed Italian Americans as synonymous with organized crime and organized crime as synonymous with Italian Americans.

Victimless crimes
Said to be those crimes which involve the willing participation of those involved in lawbreaking activities involving illegal gambling, drinking, loan-sharking, prostitution, drugs, and the like. Such a description is not always accurate, since people are often harmed by such activities and become "victims."

Volstead Act
The enforcement vehicle for Prohibition, passed on October 27, 1919, and effective on January 16, 1920. Any alcoholic beverage containing more than one-half of one percent alcohol was considered intoxicating and prohibited, although there were religious and medicinal exemptions.

A commissioner of Prohibition was created to administer the law in the Bureau of Internal Revenue.

WASP

Stands for White Anglo-Saxon Protestant.

Weiss, Earl "Hymie" (1898–1926)

Inventor of the "one-way ride," partner with Dion O'Banion, and a principal foe of Capone.

Wets

Those who stood for lax enforcement of the Prohibition laws and worked for their repeal.

White Hand Society

Group organized to combat the Black Hand Society.

Wilkerson, Judge James H.

The judge who presided over Capone's income tax trial.

Wilson, Frank J.

IRS agent picked by Elmer Irey to identify Capone's spending so as to estimate his taxable income and use it against him at his trial.

Wire Service

The means whereby bookmakers could get timely racing information, enabling setting up bookie joints that supplied horseplayers with the latest racing data such as entries, scratches, jockey changes, track conditions, the live call of the races, and any pertinent information helpful to them and the bettors.

Yale, Frankie (1885–1928)

Career gangster who gave Capone his first job with gangland, hiring him as a bouncer for the Harvard Inn in Coney Island. Yale was one of those who recommended Capone to Johnny Torrio in Chicago, but he later turned against his protégé and was killed.

Young Turks

A revolutionary group seeking change.

Zuta, Jack (d. 1930)

Whoremaster and political fixer for Capone; he turned on his boss and allied with Joe Aiello and Bugs Moran in an unsuccessful attempt to kill Capone, and paid with his life.

BIBLIOGRAPHY

BOOKS

Albini, Joseph L. *The American Mafia: Genesis of a Legend.* New York, 1971.

Allsop, Kenneth. *The Bootleggers.* London, 1961.

Asbury, Herbert. *The Barbary Coast.* New York, 1933.

————. *The French Quarter: An Informal History of the New Orleans Underworld.* New York, 1936.

————. *The Gangs of New York.* New York, 1928.

Baltzell, E. Digby. *The Protestant Establishment: Aristocracy and Caste in America.* New York, 1964.

Bell, Daniel. "Crime as an American Way of Life." *Antioch Review* (summer 1953): vol. 13, pp. 131–54.

————. *The End of Ideology.* Glencoe, 1960.

Bergreen, Laurence. *Capone: The Man and the Era.* New York, 1994.

Demaris, Ovid. *Captive City: Chicago in Chains.* New York, 1969.

Eisenberg, Dennis, Dan, Uri, and Landau, Eli. *Mayer Lansky: Mogul of the Mob.* New York, 1979.

Fonzi, Gaeton. *Annenberg: A Biography of Power.* New York, 1969.

Fox, Stephen. *Blood and Power: Organized Crime in Twentieth-Century America.* New York, 1989.

Gosch, Martin A., and Richard Hammer. *The Last Testament of Lucky Luciano.* Boston, 1974.

Ianni, Francis A. J. *A Family Business: Kinship and Social Control in Organized Crime.* New York, 1972.

Iorizzo, Luciano J. *Italian Immigration and the Impact of the Padrone System*. New York, 1980.

Iorizzo, Luciano J., and Salvatore Mondello. *The Italian Americans*. New York, 1971.

———. *The Italian Americans*. Rev. ed. Boston, 1980.

Jennings, Dean. *We Only Kill Each Other: The Incredible Story of Bugsy Siegel—Mobster*. Greenwich, Conn., 1967.

Johnson, David R. *American Law Enforcement: A History*. St. Louis, 1981.

Katcher, Leo. *The Big Bankroll: The Life and Times of Arnold Rothstein*. New Rochelle, N.Y., 1958.

Katz, Leonard. *Uncle Frank: The Biography of Frank Costello*. New York, 1973.

Kenney, Denis J., and James O. Finckenauer. *Organized Crime in America*. New York, 1995.

Kobler, John K. *Capone: The Life and World of Al Capone*. New York, 1971.

Lacey, Robert. *Little Man Meyer Lansky and the Gangster Life*. Boston, 1991.

LaGumina, Salvatore J., et al., eds. *The Italian American Experience: An Encyclopedia*. New York, 2000.

Landesco, John. *Organized Crime in Chicago*. Illinois Crime Survey, part 3. 1929. Reprint, Chicago, 1968.

Maas, Peter. *The Valachi Papers*. New York, 1968.

McPhaul, John J. *Johnny Torrio, First of the Gang Lords*. New Rochelle, 1970.

Mencken, H.L. *The American Language*, Supplement II. New York,1962.

Messick, Hank. *Lansky*. New York, 1971.

Moore, William Howard. *The Kefauver Committee and the Politics of Crime 1950–1952*. Columbia, Mo., 1974.

Morris, Norval, and Gordon Hawkins. "Organized Crime and God." In *The Honest Politicians Guide to Crime Control*. Chicago, 1970.

Nash, Jay Robert. *Bloodletters and Badmen: A Narrative Encyclopedia of American Criminals from the Pilgrims to the Present*. New York, 1973.

———. *World Encyclopedia of Organized Crime*. New York, 1993.

Nelli, Humbert S. *The Business of Crime: Italians and Syndicate Crime in the United States*. New York, 1976.

———. *The Italians of Chicago, 1880–1930: A Study in Ethnic Mobility*. New York, 1970.

Pasley, Fred D. *Al Capone: The Biography of a Self-Made Man*. 1930. Reprint, Freeport, N.Y., 1971.

Peterson, Virgil W. *Barbarians in Our Midst: A History of Chicago Crime and Politics*. Boston, 1952.

————. *The Mob: 200 Years of Organized Crime in New York*. Ottowa, Ill., 1983.

Pitkin, Thomas M., and Francesco Cordasco. *The Black Hand: A Chapter in Ethnic Crime*. Totowa, N.J., 1977.

Reid, Ed. *The Grim Reapers: The Anatomy of Organized Crime in America, City by City*. Chicago, 1970.

Reid, Ed, and Ovid Demaris. *The Green Felt Jungle*. New York, 1963.

Schoenberg, Robert J. *Mr. Capone*. New York, 2001.

Short, Martin. *Crime Inc.: The Story of Organized Crime*. London, 1984.

Sifakis, Carl. *The Encyclopedia of American Crime*. New York, 1982.

Smith, Dwight C. *The Mafia Mystique*. New York, 1975.

Sowell, Thomas. *Ethnic America: A History*. New York, 1981.

Spalding, Henry D. *Joys of Italian Humor*. New York, 1997.

Stockdale, Tom. *The Life and Times of Al Capone*. Philadelphia, 1998.

Sullivan, Richard F. "The Economics of Crime: An Introduction to the Literature." In *An Economic Analysis of Crime: Selected Readings*, by Lawrence J. Kaplan and Dennis Kessler. Springfield, Ill., 1976.

Thernstrom, Stephan, ed. *Harvard Encyclopedia of American Ethnic Groups*. Cambridge, 1980.

Turkus, Burton B., and Sid Feder. *Murder, Inc.: The Inside Story of the "Syndicate."* New York, 1972.

Ward, Geoffrey C., and Ken Burn. *Jazz: A History of America's Music*. New York, 2000.

Wendt, Lloyd, and Herman Kogan. *Bosses in Lusty Chicago: The Story of Bathhouse John and Hinky Dink*. Bloomington, Ind., 1943.

MOTION PICTURES AND VIDEOS

Al Capone. Allied Artists, 1931. Reissued, Key Video, 7750, 1986.

"Al Capone: Scarface." *Biography*. A&E Home Video, AAE-14069, 1997.

Al Capone: The Untouchable Legend. Janson, VHS 20073, 1998.

Capone. Twentieth-Century Fox, 1975. Videocassette.

Capone. Vidmark Entertainment, VM 5688, 1999.

Court TV Crime Stories Mobsters Al Capone. Unapix Home Entertainment, UPX70659, 2000.

The Gangsters: Bugsy Siegel, Dutch Schultz, and Al Capone. Rhino Home Video, 1991.

History's Mysteries: The Legacy of Al Capone. The History Channel, 2000.

La Cosa Nostra: The Mafia–An Expose: Al Capone. Madacy Entertainment Group, 1997.

Mister Scarface. Troma Team Video, VHS 4631, 1997.

The Public Enemy. Motion Picture, Warner Brothers Studios, 1931. Reissued, 2000, Warner Brothers Video 65032.

Scarface. Universal, 1932. Reissued, MCA Universal Home Video, 1991.

Scarface. Universal City Studios, 1983. DVD Widescreen, 1998.

THE INTERNET

There is a wealth of information on Al Capone and his associates available on the Internet. Select any search engine (e.g., Google or Yahoo) enter *Capone*, *Capone's car*, or the like, and a number of entries will be found. Some of the better, more useful ones include:

www.archives.gov/exhibit_hall/American_originals/capone.html

www.chicagohistory.org/history/capone/cpnbibli.html

foia.fbi.gov/capone.htm (Contains 2,379 pages of material on Capone in the files of the Federal Bureau of Investigation.)

http://search.yahoo.co./bin/search?p = movies (Will bring up Internet Movie Database [IMDb]: "everything you ever wanted to know about every movie ever made.")

www.alcaponemuseum.com (Informative and allows viewers to play "Al Capone Jeopardy" on-line in five categories: Capone the Man, Gangster Hits, The Massacre, Foes and Friends, and Around Chicago.)

www.alcatrazhistory.com

www.americanmafia.com

www.crimelibrary.com/capone

www.crimemagazine.com

www.miles-pocketwatches.com/1925_Packard.html (Contains pictures and a description of Capone's 1925 Packard-6 Cylinder Phaeton.)

www.oregoncoasttraveler.com/nwpt.html (Claims to have Capone's yacht available for tourists to view at Newport, Oregon.)

www.talesofoldchina.com/shanghai/it-capo.htm (Contains an interesting tale that describes Capone's armored car in detail.)

INDEX

About the Author

LUCIANO IORIZZO is Emeritus Professor of History at the State University of New York, Oswego.